The Promise
of
Teilhard

Also by Philip Hefner

The Scope of Grace:
   Essays in Honor of Joseph Sittler (Editor)
Faith and the Vitalities of History:
   A Theological Study Based
   on the Work of Albrecht Ritschl
The Future of the American Church (Editor)
Changing Man: The Threat and the Promise
   (Co-editor with Kyle Haselden)

The Promise of Theology
Martin E. Marty, General Editor

The Promise of Barth
The Promise of Bennett
The Promise of Bonhoeffer
The Promise of Buber
The Promise of Bultmann
The Promise of Heschel
The Promise of Kierkegaard
The Promise of H. Richard Niebuhr
The Promise of Reinhold Niebuhr
The Promise of Karl Rahner
The Promise of Teilhard
The Promise of Tillich

The Promise
of
Teilhard

The Meaning of
the Twentieth Century
in Christian Perspective

by

PHILIP HEFNER

J. B. LIPPINCOTT COMPANY
Philadelphia and New York

To

Neva, Sarah, Martha, and Julia

Foreword

Within ten years after Teilhard de Chardin had been known only as a sometimes suppressed and always suspect Jesuit, he had become one of the most touted and most followed of modern thinkers. Societies of devotees in France, America, and elsewhere held conferences and symposia, published journals, scraped up and released his literary legacy, and debated his role as the prophet of the future. Detractors also arose, some dismissing him as a charlatan and others faulting him either for his mystical approach to science or for an heretical approach to Christianity. Somewhere between these extremes of extravagant devotion and vehement condemnation a "real" Teilhard lives on—as he does in this book.

Professor Hefner provides a distinctive focus on the late priest by locating him as the newest-fangled representative of an old-fashioned category, that of the Christian humanist. The author clearly believes that Christians need models for such humanism today and can find them in Teilhard, among others. It is apparent that, for Hefner, Christians have no place to go if they do not come to terms with scientific-humanist striving in our day, and that Christian theology must find a new center in the possibilities offered by evolutionary and developmental processes. Teilhard is not his only guide; men like the philosopher Alfred North Whitehead have also set precedents. But Teilhard's peculiar devotion and his style of life help him serve as a pioneer and pathfinder.

In a day when vision is sought and when people urgently seek "alternative futures," Hefner presents Teilhard as a man in advance of us who speaks of a God in advance of us. Since he is a futuristic thinker, Teilhard deserves to be tested in the light of the concept of "promise." As he meets those tests, he offers us both promise and challenge.

MARTIN E. MARTY
The University of Chicago

[5]

Preface

The discussion of Teilhard de Chardin that follows in this essay is largely determined by a well-defined and preconceived understanding of what his *promise* is for those of us who live in the generation after his. I have not set out to "introduce" the man as such, nor have I undertaken a balanced analysis of every aspect of his thought. To have entered upon either venture would have taken much more space than this short essay affords. Rather, I have seized upon those facets of his life and writing that seem to hold particular promise for our generation, and I have included only as much introduction and analysis as is necessary to sustain my discussion.

This approach produces a picture of Teilhard that I characterize as the Christian humanist, a Teilhard who was absorbed in the effort to discern the meaning of the age in which he lived; consequently, my study of Teilhard moves the volume of essays that has appeared under the title *The Future of Man* into a pivotal position for interpreting his thought. This picture of the man will seem strange to the reader who has thought of Teilhard chiefly as a Christian theologian, because it subordinates his theology and puts it in the service of the larger quest for the meaning of our time. By subordinating his theology to his Christian humanism, the present study touches upon one of the great dilemmas of Teilhard study. Teilhard is sometimes counted in the company of professional theologians, primarily because the technical theological controversies that swirled about him long before he was internationally known as a scientist or a spiritual figure inevitably assumed that he *was* a theologian. The controversies received wider publicity than his works themselves, which were largely under the ban. Since his first opponents were professional theologians, and thus determined that his first defenders would be of the same fraternity, it is understandable that the theological dimensions of his thought have received the most exhaustive technical analysis. But the flurry raised by the professionals and the bias of their Teilhard analysis should not be permitted to obscure the fact that Teilhard was by profession neither a theologian nor an ecclesiastical functionary. The judgment of Professor Georges Crespy deserves close attention: "Teilhard never developed a theological system in and for itself. A Teilhardian catechism does not exist. Indeed, in the technical sense of the term a Teilhardian theology does not even exist."[1]*

Teilhard's work defies compartmentalizing by academic disciplines or theological schools. As Chapter I explains in detail, it is the work of a man who comes on as a full-orbed human being in all of his writing, and it is precisely the kind of achievement that is the most difficult for academics and professionals to understand, since they are wont to reduce him to the shape and size dictated by their familiar categories. Teilhard was a towering spiritual figure, engaged throughout his lifetime in paleontological research, thoroughly Christian and specifically Jesuit. His thought holds great significance for the theologian, it is true, but it is also pertinent to the scientist, and, perhaps even more, to mankind generally. As the study unfolds, the reader will understand why I have tried to express Teilhard's breadth with the phrase "Christian humanism."

The perspective I have employed holds the disadvantage that it tends to slight the theological complexities of Teilhard's work and the controversies that have grown up around him. I hope that these drawbacks are counterbalanced by certain advantages: (a) that Teilhard's own disclaimers to doing technical theology can be accepted at face value; (b) that we can take more fully into account his tremendous popularity today among those who are not professional theologians; (c) that we can free ourselves from the task of supplying theological clarity and consistency where he himself did not or could not; (d) that a fresh perspective can be opened up for appreciating certain facets of Teilhard's work that are often obscured.

I have made a conscious effort not to involve the reader in the scholarly controversies that attend Teilhard's thought, even though I do indicate the areas in which there is disagreement about his meaning. These indications, together with references in the notes and bibliography, should enable the reader to get a balanced impression.

The reader will note that I have preferred to include assessment and critique of Teilhard within the body of the study, thereby carrying on a running dialogue with his thought, rather than drawing such material

*Superior figures refer to the Notes at the end of the text.

together in a final chapter. At every point, I have sought to focus on the promise of the man for the present generation, assessing his work in terms of its viability for our own quest after meaning in our time.

PHILIP HEFNER
*Lutheran School of Theology
at Chicago*

Contents

I

Pierre Teilhard de Chardin—
Fully Man

How does one classify him? Perhaps that is the most difficult task of all, and the one that raises the most serious obstacles to understanding what he has to say to us. How can we hope to grasp the promise of a man's life and work if we cannot classify him intelligibly?

Born in 1881 into a patrician home on the ancestral estate in Auvergne, France, nurtured on Sacred Heart of Jesus piety, Marie-Joseph-Pierre Teilhard de Chardin was by temperament and training a Jesuit. At age forty-one, after service for his order in Egypt and for his country in World War I, he won a doctorate from the Sorbonne in paleontology, "with very honorable mention," and seemed to have a bright university career ahead of him. His advanced ideas and his abilities to articulate those ideas before large audiences whom his charm and earnestness attracted got him into difficulties with his ecclesiastical superiors. From the time he turned forty-three, ecclesiastical edict and the Japanese invasion of China kept him away from France for all of his remaining thirty-one years save a brief interlude immediately after World War II. Most of his "exile" was spent in China, where circumstance brought him to a leading position on the international team of scientists that discovered the fossil remains of Peking Man. That same exile took him, eventually, to every important site associated with prehistoric human life that was known in his day. The last three and one half years of his life were spent in the United States, where his office and residence were near Central Park, New York. He died in New York on Easter Sunday, 1955. A dozen or so attended his funeral, and two fellow Jesuits accompanied his body to the Jesuit novitiate at St. Andrews-on-Hudson, where he lies buried.

He was a brilliant Jesuit paleontologist, whose very life and career were determined by ecclesiastical ban. Although he sought to explain in detail the relationship between his religious faith and his scientific work and wrote extensively on the implications of his scientific work for Christian faith, his order prohibited him from publishing any except his purely scientific treatises. Apart from the private distribution of his essays, very few of his important philosophical and religious works saw the light of day until his friends published them after his death.

Since his death, one leading British scientist, P. B. Medawar, has written that Teilhard's major work, *The Phenomenon of Man*, "is nonsense tricked out in a variety of metaphysical conceits," and as recently as May, 1969, the *New York Times* book reviewer used the appearance of a new volume of Teilhard's letters as an occasion for heaping scorn on the speculations of Teilhard's system of thought. Another British scientist, Julian Huxley, who was also one of Teilhard's closest friends in his later years, wrote the preface to *The Phenomenon of Man*. Ecclesiastically, Teilhard's influence is massive. There are those who insist that he was a dominant force in the Second Vatican Council. At many Catholic universities, the study of his works is standard fare for graduate students in theology. Meanwhile, quite apart from either church or university, there are Teilhard "associations" on five continents and several "Teilhard journals," published in English, French, and German. The president of the American Teilhard de Chardin Association is the internationally renowned geneticist, Theodosius Dobzhansky. The various Teilhard "newsletters" reveal that Teilhard study conferences were held last year in many parts of the world, including both the Isle of Jersey, on the south coast of Britain, where Teilhard once studied, and at the College of Air Warfare in Manby, England, for senior NATO and Royal Air Force officers. The same sources tell of a teacher who has developed a "Montessorian-Teilhardian approach" to child education, of courses taught on Teilhard's thought in high schools, of films being made to elaborate on Teilhard's vision of the world, and of a discussion at the Bell Telephone Laboratories in Chester, New Jersey, in which twenty-five scientists considered "the place of telecommunications in a Teilhardian universe." The Dean of Araneta University in the Philippines writes that the ninety-four members of the Teilhard study group there "feel that Teilhard's writings have special significance in relation to the present Far Eastern crisis." The 1969 official archives of the Society of Jesus reveal that "never in the history of the Society has so much been written about one of its sons." Since 1963, for example, of 4,591 indexed articles and books on Jesuit figures, 1,188 deal with Teilhard. Finally, Marxist thinkers have devoted considerable attention to Teilhard, exemplified earlier this year when *Cronica,* a weekly journal published in Romania, devoted an entire issue to him. And yet, the *Encyclopedia Britannica* recently decided to give only briefest mention to Teilhard, on the grounds that his popularity is "only a passing fad."

How to classify him? The bare facts alone of who Teilhard was and what he is today defy an easy answer to this question. For his critics, classification of Teilhard amounts to a nosology—the labeling of diseases both scientific and theological. For those on the other extreme, it amounts to a piety or veneration. As we might expect, the classification of Teilhard has been synonymous with interpreting him. Those who have consigned him to metaphysics have felt free to disregard the scientific thrust of his thought, while those who see him as a mystic are inclined to look with indifference at his philosophical significance. For still others, his alleged theological inadequacies are excused because he is a "natural theologian."

It is necessary, in the light of this confusion, to look more carefully at the man and his work and trace more precisely the reasons why he is so difficult to place. At the very outset, when we approach this man, Pierre Teilhard de Chardin, we are confronted with considerable confusion as to the genre of his work. As we shall see, the praise and the criticism he has received have been closely tied to the particular pigeonhole in which his readers have placed him. As biographer Robert Speaight has observed, "Between the smoke raised by his critics and the smoke raised by his thurifers his true stature tends to be obscured."[1]

The difficulties in determining the genre of Teilhard's work, and hence its significance, are rooted in Teilhard himself, in the purposes he set for himself and in the particular style of life that he fashioned. At the risk of cliché, let us say that Teilhard was fully man, as well as an integrated man, and his work corresponds to the man that he was.

He was *fully man,* in that he was open to a wide range of human experiences—perhaps as wide a range as any single human life could encompass—and he welcomed those experiences. A patrician, he had known the benefits of an upper-class education and home life; his maternal lineage included Voltaire, and his father's discipline included attention to the fascinating natural surroundings of the estate in Auvergne as well as personally supervised Latin lessons and reading lists from classics in world literature in the years before the children attended school. As a medic in the 8th regiment of Tunisian sharpshooters, he not only served his time during the First World War but served with distinction, earning his decorations for special bravery, including the impressive feat of retrieving the body of a friend who had fallen only feet from the German front lines and carrying it on his back for hours before returning to his own lines. A celibate by conviction and propensity, he nevertheless came to terms with sexuality; he was a confidant of noted women, including France's most prominent feminist, Léontine Zanta. He could write, "It seems to me beyond dispute that however devoted a man may be to the service of a cause or a God ..., he can no more do without the feminine than he can do without light or oxygen." The depths of religious experience were probed by Teilhard the mystic, just as the realms of intellectual brilliance were his domain. His doctoral dissertation on the mammifers of the Lower Eocene period in France had been preceded by a dozen scientific papers that had grown out of his work in France, Belgium, England, and Egypt; France bestowed its highest honors upon him—the rank of Officer in the Order of the Legion of Honor, membership in the Académie des Sciences, and the offer of a chair at the Collège de France (which his order did not permit him to accept). Another side of Teilhard's full manhood is shown in the priceless photographs in the *Teilhard de Chardin Album* that Mmes. Mortier and Auboux have collected—the rugged wastes of the Gobi desert, the thousands of miles through wild, scarcely populated territory that Teilhard traversed in China—and not, we should remember, as a tourist, but as an explorer and leader of expeditions who was frequently charged with the responsibility of supervising dozens of fellow workers. Teilhard was a man at home in Paris' finest salons, and he traveled in France's most prestigious intellectual circles. But he also pitched his tent and cooked his own food for weeks at a time on pack trips across Asia's midsection.

Teilhard was an *integrated man,* in that he brought his full being, in all its dimensions, to bear in all that he did. He stands as the very antithesis of the "compartmentalized man," who separates his left-hand activities from his right. He was a scientific specialist, and he won his place on expeditionary task forces, such as the team which worked on Peking Man and in the Cenozoic Research Laboratory, a division of the prewar China Geological Survey, because of the specialized competence he could contribute. He was also an educated theologian, who, although he possessed no advanced degrees in theology, had passed the rigors of a Jesuit religious education, under first-rate teachers, in the company of peers who went on to become leading theologians and philosophers. His religious "education" was linked to

[16]

an authentic piety of such depth that Teilhard can be classed as a true mystic, for whom all of life and reality was a vehicle of religious insight and divine revelation. Finally, and not so widely acknowledged, he was an alert observer of his times, with a restless curiosity into the meaning of the events that he lived through in the epoch that spanned the closing days of the nineteenth century on the one hand and the explosion of the atomic bomb and the founding of the United Nations on the other. And this wide-ranging human being was endowed with an articulateness and a facility with language, not uncommon to the French theological scene, that ranks him with the best masters of his native tongue. It was this gift of expression that made it possible for him to popularize both his scientific ideas and his religious visions.

Because Teilhard's work corresponds to the fullness and integrity of his manhood, it has perplexed his interpreters. At two poles, the "purely" scientific and the "purely" mystical, we should expect Teilhard's thinking and writing to be clearly classifiable and understandable within the limits of those genres. This assessment is accurate of the first group of writings, the purely scientific treatises in geology, paleontology, and the like, the articles that appeared, for example, in the bulletins of the French Geological Society, the Chinese Geological Society, and the Belgian Royal Academy. But these articles—with such technical-sounding titles as "On a Presumably Pleistocene Human Tooth from the Sjara-Osso-Gol Deposits" and "On the Occurrence of a Mongolian Eocene Perissodactyle in the Red Sandstone of Sichuan, S.W. Honan," approximately two hundred such titles altogether—are seldom read nowadays, since they are largely superseded and have made their contribution to the later researches of Teilhard's successors. These scientific works, which account for 40 per cent of Teilhard's written work, are not included in the official *Complete Works* that have been published by the Fondation Teilhard de Chardin or in the English translations of Teilhard's works. Even if they were easily available, only the specialist could assess their significance and meaning—and they would hardly give us a full picure of the man!

No other segment of his work and thought is as unambiguous or clearly specialized as the scientific work. Even his mystical writings, at their most ecstatic and adorational, such as "The Mass on the World," "Christ in the World of Matter," and the prayers in *The Divine Milieu,* show the traces of his scientific commitments which rendered them puzzling or objectionable to his Catholic contemporaries. The works

[17]

between these two poles are synthetic writings that defy classification. The popularizations of scientific findings *(The Vision of the Past, The Appearance of Man)* include the brilliant and controversial interpretations which betray Teilhard's philosophical and theological assumptions. The vast synthetic works (including his masterwork, *The Phenomenon of Man,* and the shorter and more recent restatement of its thesis, *Man's Place in Nature)* bring to bear every one of Teilhard's many sides. Finally, the essays in which Teilhard expresses his observations of current events assume both his scientific and his theological perspectives, so that they are the most pungent and the most controversial pieces that he wrote (for example, *The Future of Man* and *Science and Christ).*

Ian Barbour has given us a useful discussion both of how Teilhard brought his whole being to his writing and of the ensuing puzzlement, in his interpretation of *The Phenomenon of Man* which he entitles "Five Ways of Reading Teilhard."[2] He brings four perspectives to this work and demonstrates how some interpreters have used each as the key to Teilhard's meaning: evolutionary science, poetry and mysticism, natural theology, and Christian theology. Barbour sees validity in these perspectives, but he advances a fifth mode of interpretation, that which sees Teilhard as a "process philosopher," in the train of Bergson and Whitehead. Let us consider in detail why Teilhard's work is open to such a diversity of interpretations.

As we shall see, Teilhard embraced without reservation what we might call a "scientific world view," and his commitment to it became integral to his elaboration of his Christian faith. Although he had a number of fellow priests among his acquaintance who agreed fully with his scientific commitments, and some teachers also, both his order and the French Catholic church were largely of a Vatican I mentality, and as a consequence they were puzzled and offended by his efforts to relate science and faith. His closest friends in the order, classmates from the early days in Jersey, Pierre Charles and Auguste Valensin, who held important chairs at Louvain and Lyons, respectively, suffered from Vatican censure as early as 1920. Thomistic philosophy was the rage, under the impact of Maritain, who was influencing a large number of conversions to the Roman Catholic Church in the twenties.

Teilhard's use of evolution as a fundamental motif for his thinking was at the core of his difficulties with his ecclesiastical superiors. In November, 1924, he was for the first time summoned by his Provincial to account for his views on original sin. A lecture he had delivered in

1922 on that topic was forwarded, under somewhat suspicious circumstances, to Rome. This was but the first of a series of objections raised by "orthodox" theologians and ecclesiastical superiors that Teilhard's thought underestimated the gravity of sin and evil. Indeed, evolutionary schemes of thought do give this impression, inasmuch as the very concept of evolution implies a continuum or process, whereas sin and evil have connoted the disruption and even the destruction of the process, whether that process be the movement of God's plan or man's progress. Teilhard's confidence that life had developed for millions of years prior to man, culminating at this point in the human species, and that it would continue for millions more, bringing the world to new stages of development, rendered it very difficult for him to consider any fundamental disruption or destruction of the process. Rather, he went to considerable lengths to speak of sin and evil as "necessary flaws in the universe," as the price that progress in the evolutionary scale must pay, as the persistent companion to all living ventures. Later this problem was to plague him so severely that he added a postscript on evil to *The Phenomenon of Man,* in the vain hope that it would move the authorities to approve the publication of the work. This particular brush with the censors brought with it the demand that Teilhard "promise that he would neither say nor write anything against the traditional position of the Church on the matter of original sin."[3] He finally, after much inner turmoil, submitted to the demand and returned to China.

Teilhard's evolutionary perspective also impelled him toward a synthesis of spiritual and material realities. What we designate as "spirit" in man has evolved under material conditions; in fact, for Teilhard, spirit is a form of matter—a highly complex form. When we consider how closely man's spirit has been related to the spirit of God in Christian theology, and how intimately Teilhard's view entwines God's creative and redemptive activity with the material world, we can understand that some Christians would be inclined to say that Teilhard depreciates the transcendent or "otherworldly" character of God and spirit.

Churchmen who were offended by Teilhard's motifs were inclined to label him as a deviationist or even a heretic. Pius XII's encyclical, *Humani Generis,* was aimed in part against Teilhard. In 1962, the Sacred Congregation of the Holy Office issued a *Monitum* (warning) against him. For this group of interpreters, Teilhard was an erratic and inadequate theologian, a theologian whose work did not hold up under judgment by the criteria of orthodoxy and methodology that were customarily applied to theologians. Some theologians have rushed to Teilhard's defense. Perhaps the most notable are Claude Tresmontant, Henri de Lubac, and Christopher Mooney. At times they argue that Teilhard is very intentionally doing apologetic theology, aimed at bringing the unbeliever, who accepts science, into the Christian frame of reference. He concentrates on the propositions which the agnostic already accepts. As a result, he cannot be rebuked for slanting his presentations in a way that would not be the case if he were writing for the fraternity of orthodox theologians. This really makes Teilhard a "natural" theologian—that is, a theologian who seeks to convince his reader of God's existence and the cogency of the Christian faith from evidences that exist in nature itself, or by persuasive reasoning, rather than from the "revealed" sources of Scripture and dogma that convince only those who already accept the faith. These defenders of Teilhard argue that he maintains a formal allegiance to the orthodox position, even if he does weight his actual writing in one direction or another. This defense is persuasive when one considers that heresy has generally been a matter of overemphasis or underemphasis on particular items of belief, rather than utter apostasy. In any case, much depends on which pigeonhole the interpreter chooses to place Teilhard in: conventional theologian or apologetic and natural theologian. Mooney accounts for this diversity of interpretations by noting the differences that exist within the interpreters themselves:

> Whether one is favourable or hostile . . . will depend in large measure upon one's theological temperament and education, one's susceptibility to change, and above all one's awareness of modern currents of thought in scientific and humanistic circles outside the Church.[4]

The diversity of interpretations of Teilhard is not rooted only in the propensities of his theological critics, however. It is also grounded in the kinds of things that the man himself said about his work. A great deal has been written, for example, about the first sentence of Teilhard's own preface to *The Phenomenon of Man:* "If this book is to be properly understood, it must be read not as a work on metaphysics, still less as a sort of theological essay, but purely and simply as a scientific treatise." Similar statements recur throughout *The Future of Man* and *Science and Christ*. There are those who defend this statement, in contrast to those who insist that these works are both metaphysics and theology, and those few who, like Medawar and the *Times* reviewer, suspect that they are nonsense. Those who are concerned to defend them as science are inclined to make a number of distinctions—between the nonscientific and the unscientific (the latter referring to what is definitely contrary to scientific knowledge) and between work that is exclusively scientific and that which contains scientific value, yet goes beyond it to include much more.

George Gaylord Simpson, the American paleontologist, asserts the nonscientific character of Teilhard's work; since Teilhard was *"primarily* a Christian mystic," his work can be neither validated nor invalidated by scientific method. Dobzhansky, in contrast, even as he maintains a critical stance toward Teilhard and calls attention to Teilhard's mysticism and poetic inspiration, goes to considerable length to defend the fundamental soundness of Teilhard's scientific statements. Teilhard's thought embraced a number of components, says Dobzhansky, of which science is one essential component, but not the only one; the other components "do not conform to the patterns of thought of the scientific community . . . but it is nevertheless important that these other components are also not contradictory to any scientifically established facts or to scientific theories generally considered as valid."[5] Others, Henri de Lubac, Robert Faricy, and Robert Francoeur, argue that Teilhard is doing "generalized science"—that is, general scientific theory that is not "subject to demonstration or verification under controlled conditions," but rather science in a "wider sense."

Teilhard *was* a scientist, and some of his writings, even apart from the two hundred scholarly paleontological and geological articles, are intelligible as such. But the main body of his influential work is obviously not what he said of his masterwork, "purely and simply" scientific. If it were, there would not be so much argument about it, with renowned scientists calling it theological mysticism and theologians calling it "generalized science." This much is clear, however: his work includes at many points a wealth of scientific data and theory, and his general theories are consistent with scientific fact and at times (as the next chapter will show) even extrapolations from that fact.

Why did Teilhard insist that his masterwork, and much of his other work as well, was "purely" scientific? It may well be, as we have just pointed out, that he meant to emphasize that his work was consistent with scientific fact, a kind of larger generalization or extrapolation based on his scientific research. There is also some evidence, however, that Teilhard was explicitly avoiding the labels of theology and metaphysics that the public would naturally place upon his work. From the most practical point of view, since the ecclesiastical censors had insisted that he publish *only* his scientific articles, in distinction from his theological and religious ideas, it would be in his own interest for Teilhard to emphasize the scientific components of his thinking. On the other hand, its basic character was alien to the kind of metaphysics and theology that Teilhard was acquainted with through his education.

Teilhard's thinking, even his most religiously oriented efforts, was consistent with scientific fact in the sense that he acknowledged the validity of his scientific thinking to criticize and shape his generalizations. In this sense, his thinking was inductive—it was, as we shall see, very much in the nature of an extrapolation, even if mystical, from the concrete world. And Teilhard's perception of that concrete world was irrevocably shaped by a scientific world view. The theology and metaphysics which Teilhard had grown up with did not permit themselves to be criticized by scientific ideas that grew out of inductive studies. Rather, they were inclined to argue deductively from certain presupposed articles of revealed truth in Scripture and dogma, "explicitating" what was believed to be in those articles. Or, as one observer has said, that theology was based on an "a priori set of abstractions."

Even if Teilhard's work as a whole is not as strictly scientific in character as the geological articles he published in the bulletins of the learned societies, it is not difficult to see why he abhorred the designation of his work as "metaphysical." To be metaphysical in the deductive sense that he was familiar with was to cut the very nerve of the methodology that was central to his thought. Dobzhansky observes that "Teilhard's religion was that of a great thinker who was aware that he lived in an age of science."[6] This meant that he had to make a concerted effort to distinguish his thought from a theology and metaphysics that was essentially prescientific in its origins, methodology, and form of presentation.

As understandable as this may be, it does not make the task of interpreting Teilhard any easier. His work includes ideas and conceptions that are almost unintelligible except as metaphysics—for example, his elaboration of the all-encompassing character of evolutionary process, his theories of the goal of evolution, and his images of the final consummation of the world. Those interpreters who, like Father Faricy, seem to operate with the same understanding of metaphysics as Teilhard did, as a deductive enterprise beginning from a priori abstractions, stretch the concept of science to almost impossible lengths to accommodate Teilhard's concepts. Faricy can thus conclude that it is futile to argue whether Teilhard was a metaphysician, because "he certainly did not think he was, and he was a philosopher only in the broad sense of one who takes a global view of reality."[7]

Outside the traditional metaphysical theological circles in which Teilhard and many of his interpreters were educated, however, there grew up a tradition of metaphysics that styled itself "descriptive," and it proceeded with considerable methodological care to make its generalizations on the basis of the concrete interpretations that are furnished by scientific research. This is the tradition of S. C. Alexander, Henri Bergson (who influenced Teilhard greatly), and Alfred North Whitehead, which attempts to elaborate the most fundamental principles of being that must be drawn in order to make sense of the data that confront us in the concrete world. Professor Ian Barbour has argued at length that, when metaphysics is defined in the tradition of Whitehead rather than in the tradition in which Teilhard grew up, the metaphysical character of Teilhard's intellectual achievement is clarified. Barbour's thesis is that Teilhard shares both Whitehead's method and his substantial concern for process or temporality as a fundamental characteristic of reality. Thus, he can write, "I conclude, then, that Teilhard's most significant intellectual contribution is a *process theology* which combines Christian theology and process philosophy."[8]

Teilhard possessed, furthermore, the stylistic ability and imagination that prompted him to employ vivid poetic images, even when he was in the midst of a technical scientific or philosophical discussion. This style has delighted some readers and infuriated others, but in either case it has added to the difficulties of judging his work. He speaks of the "new man" who has emerged in our time, for example, as a "new substance" that appeared in the "heart of the thinking magma," or of the increase of complexity as a "heating up" and "incandescence." He is fond of using physical and chemical terms to apply to psychic phenomena. Naturally, this raises the question of whether Teilhard was consciously stretching language and concepts to make his points or whether he really did believe that the imagistic style was appropriate to the objects he discussed.

The threads of interpretation are thus exceedingly knotted: (1) If we accept his own disclaimers, much of his work seems contradictory, hopelessly metaphysical and theological and mystical, unlike the scientific articles we read on occasion. (2) If we place him in the camp of the metaphysicians and theologians with whom he was acquainted and by whom many of his current interpreters were educated, we open him up to criticism by a deductive methodology and "orthodoxy" that is foreign to his work. (3) If we seek to avoid the imposition of alien metaphysical categories upon his work by accepting his own claims to be "purely" scientific, we must stretch the use of the term science or introduce a concept of "phenomenology" that really is not useful, because it must deviate so far from conventional uses of those terms. (4) If we discount Teilhard's own statements and introduce a different metaphysical-theological tradition, we can make sense of much of his work, although, to be sure, in an exclusively intellectual perspective that admittedly disregards his mystical dimension and the immense influence he has exerted on Christian piety or spirituality. (5) If we interpret him solely in terms of his mystical and poetic religious inspiration, we blind ourselves to the lifelong effort of his scientific and intellectual endeavors, which he considered integral to his religious life.

A man who was less concerned to bring his full manhood and his integrity of being to bear upon his work and thought, who was more concerned with the niceties of intellectual and academic specialization, would be easier to understand. There is yet one final obstacle to interpreting Teilhard that figures large in any attempt to understand him fairly and accurately—an obstacle that is a function of the person he was and the life he lived. Because Teilhard suffered from the prohibition against publishing his most important works, these works were privately duplicated and circulated, some of the time in a form he did not authorize. His works underwent several revisions, with different drafts of each revision circulating simultaneously! Some drafts were prepared for publication, while other drafts of the same article were purposely revised with an eye for the audience that they were likely to find, and still others were purely personal copies, representing a tentative form that Teilhard meant only for himself and the comment of his closest friends. It is not difficult to imagine the herculean task that confronted (and still burdens) the committee of friends and other experts that has undertaken to edit and publish Teilhard's complete works.

The isolation which ecclesiastical censure imposed upon Teilhard meant, in addition, that he could not count on the kind of criticism and broad discussion of his work that comes from publication and extended debate with critics. Anyone who has attempted to articulate an idea can appreciate the pain and uncertainty that Teilhard must have known when he had to send out his essays and books as solitary trial balloons, certain only of their reading by friends whose opinions he knew too well and censors whom he never succeeded in persuading.

As a consequence of these difficulties, there is no full set of Teilhard's works in print. Even some of the most important essays are unavailable. A good deal of what has been edited in French is in English translation, most of it reliable, although some few volumes have been issued in translations of questionable quality.

There are at least two good biographies available, Claude Cuénot's *Teilhard de Chardin* and Robert Speaight's *The Life of Teilhard de Chardin,* but neither is definitive in character. From time to time, there are indications that the intense loyalty and affection which his friends hold for Teilhard has compromised somewhat the quality of their editing of his works. Arthur Knodel, Professor of French at the University of Southern California, writes, for example, that although there is no question that Teilhard was a Catholic Christian by both inclination and decision, "it does seem to me that the complete and uninterrupted serenity of Teilhard's faith, on which his apologists somewhat stridently insist, is open to serious question."9 He goes on to quote fragments of letters in which a picture of Teilhard's doubts and inner anxieties is hinted at. Knodel complains that the editions of his letters "are unfailingly irritating because the letters are almost never quoted *in toto,* and the reader has no real clue as to the nature of the materials omitted . . . I do not think that even the most uncritical of Teilhard's admirers have anything to fear" from a truly critical edition of Teilhard's letters.10 It seems strange that, even at this late date, Emile Rideau, in his recent comprehensive survey and summary of Teilhard's thought, gives no information concerning Teilhard's difficulties with ecclesiastical authority.

That Teilhard was thoroughly a religious and a scientist is beyond all doubt. His career was both religious and scientific, just as his fundamental view of life and all of reality was inwardly shaped and outwardly articulated by both the religious and the scientific ethos in which he lived. As indisputable as this may be, one wonders, nevertheless, whether Teilhard should be left to either the theologians or the scientists. One wonders whether either the scientific or the religious community has understood him aright and presented him properly to the world. The geneticist Theodosius Dobzhansky, who himself defies compartmentalization, has written:

Nothing like the Teilhardian synthesis could have been attempted by anyone lacking a first-hand familiarity with science. Yet Teilhard makes it abundantly clear that his message is addressed to the whole of mankind, not to scientists alone.[11]

A comparable statement could be framed with respect to Teilhard's Christian religious commitments. In his thinking, Teilhard forged a fullness and integrity of vision that corresponds to the unity of his life and work as a person. It was this wholeness of vision, this synthesis, that he was intent upon communicating in his writings, just as he was intent upon embodying it in his life. The Teilhardian vision or synthesis was scientific because Teilhard himself was inwardly shaped by the scientific world view; it was religious and Christian for the same reason. But no matter how intrinsic and irreplaceable these dimensions are to the man and his thought, the logic and intention of his thought are ruptured if he is subsumed under analytical categories that overlook his wholeness. It is for this reason, no doubt, that his work and memory have awakened such a broad nonspecialized appeal—from the College of Air Warfare to the Bell Telephone scientists and the Montessori schoolteacher.

But do we really know how to understand and interpret the thought of a man who comes on with the wholeness of a Teilhard? Do we have the grace and skills to show proper hospitality to his achievement? Another author, Victor Ferkiss, a political scientist who has also attempted a synthesis on a large scale, has given us a clue to the problem in a description of his own work:

To study politics today—and especially to study the politics of tomorrow—is to study all aspects of human life. In an era when academic specialization and ethical abdication are the hallmarks of virtue, any kind of interdisciplinary study centered on normative concerns opens one to reproach from many quarters—from those whose self-imposed limitations have been abandoned and those whose territory has been invaded, from those who view concern with values as a sign of approaching senility and those who simply regard your values as the wrong ones. But if one takes the task of the social scientist seriously, one must go where the problems are, and if one acts as a human being as well as a scientist, one must go where the relevant problems are. The result is a book that, because it is about everything, can be definitive about nothing; but one hopes it may help set readers on the track of the real issues facing mankind today.[12]

With a few words changed, this could have been written by Teilhard or about him—and, raised to a higher level than Professor Ferkiss intended it, it is an accurate statement of Teilhard's intentions and the difficulties he encountered in expressing his vision to the world.

I suggest that the key to interpreting Teilhard lies in a paragraph he wrote in 1942:

> During recent years I have sought in a long series of essays [he mentions his major works here], not to philosophize in the Absolute, but as a naturalist or physicist to discover a general significance in the events in which we are materially involved. A great many internal and external portents (political and social upheaval, moral and religious unease) have caused us all to feel, more or less confusedly, that something tremendous is at present taking place in the world. But what is it? (FM, 82).*

"As a naturalist to discover a general significance in the events in which we are materially involved." Is this science? theology? mysticism? metaphysics? The answer to each is "Yes. And yet more." It is more to the point to say that Teilhard's intentions were fundamentally human. He was a full human being of great intelligence, discipline, and sensitivity who, from a scientific and Christian perspective, sought to make sense of the events through which he was living and communicate that sense or vision to the world.

How then does one go about assessing and interpreting such an enterprise as Teilhard's? Of course, it would be absurd to deny the theologian or the biologist or the paleontologist or the historian his right to scrutinize Teilhard's vision according to the methods and criteria of his specialized field of expertise. The verdicts from these specialized fields are of importance in understanding and evaluating Teilhard. But as we know very well, from our experience in attempting to understand human beings and societies, one may analyze many of the individual features and still not comprehend the whole in a satisfactory way. It is important to know that Franklin Delano Roosevelt suffered from polio, or that Martin Luther may have had severe psychological problems, or that John F. Kennedy was both Irish Catholic and from the upper social and economic class, but such

*A Key to Abbreviations appears at the end of the text.

specialized information is only partially helpful in understanding the total impact and significance of these men.

Teilhard may perhaps be best understood as a man who built a number of comprehensive theories or "models" for the purpose of clarifying the meaning of the contemporary history he was living through. The enterprise of building models is a risky and uncertain one, because models are built for the purpose of explaining what has not previously been explained. A new model cannot be tested exhaustively by our present knowledge and understanding, because its very purpose is to open up new meanings of facts that are already available. In this context, I use the term "model" to refer to an image of thought that suggests the fundamental nature of whatever it refers to. The only final test of a model is its ability to make sense of the material it deals with. A physicist's model for understanding the phenomenon of light—for example, whether light is composed of waves or particles—can only be judged by its ability to make coherent sense of everything the physicist knows about light.

When we transpose the model-building task to Teilhard's purpose, the interpretation of contemporary history, we sense immediately the magnitude of the task and the ambiguities that attend it. A model which purports to "discover a general significance" in the contemporary events he lived through must be nothing less that a global image. And when we say that the ultimate test of its promise or validity is its capacity to make coherent sense of current history, we are stepping into very uncertain territory indeed. But we are at least putting the issue in the way that Teilhard intended. When we consider, furthermore, that Teilhard was thinking of a "significance" that included the very first beginnings and the very last endings of our universe, it is clear that we are dealing with an interpreter of current events on a grand scale—one who stands with colleagues like Hegel, Spengler, Toynbee, and Marcuse.

II

"A General Significance in Events"

When we say that Teilhard seeks to interpret the contemporary history that he was living through, we mean that he was seeking an interpretation that would relate current history to the most fundamental realities imaginable—to the basic process of life, to the very beginnings and endings of history, to God himself. He is to be compared with an Oswald Spengler, who interpreted the events of the first half of the twentieth century as proof that Western civilization was running down, or an Arnold Toynbee, who has discerned the basic rhythm of civilization as challenge and response. Teilhard's wide-ranging interpretations of the direction of events were confined to magazines and journals of less than mass appeal, but nevertheless they were nontechnical and very influential among the more educated classes of people. Some of the most important of these articles are collected in *The Future of Man* and *Science and Christ;* their contents are integrated into *The Phenomenon of Man* and *Man's Place in Nature.*

Those who did read Teilhard's articles in the intellectual Catholic journals found that he created his own vocabulary to make his analyses and drive home his points. Of course, he was not the first thinker who felt obliged to exasperate his readers by writing his own dictionary of terms, but few have given birth to more verbal offspring than he. The Protestant reader, however, may find it pleasant to enter the world of new terms formed from the French, as a relief from the Germanisms that have plagued so much of his own theology. Teilhard's need to create new words is puzzling to the reader who approaches him for the first time. He has a habit of applying suffixes and prefixes, for example, to make new forms. Three of his most important prefixes are "hyper," "ultra," and "super," as in "ultrahuman" or "superhuman." These prefixes carry the implication of *intensifying* and *perfecting,* particularly in the realm of the spirit. Thus, the "superhumanizing" process is the process of man's development toward the most intense and perfect actualization of his personality and his solidarity with his fellow men. These prefixes refer more to an increase in quality than in quantity. An important suffix for Teilhard is "genesis," as in "cosmogenesis," "anthropogenesis," and "Christogenesis." By this term, Teilhard wished to convey that the world, man, Christ, or whatever entity he referred to was not a static reality, but rather a dynamic reality in the process of change and development. He would not say that the universe "is," but rather that the universe has *come to be* through a process that is still going on. Thus, he would use the term "cosmogenesis" to express the idea.

A. Planetization: Teilhard's First Extrapolation

As Teilhard grew older, he developed great powers of crystallizing his fundamental vision in very few words. It is true that one ought not forego reading the great work of his life, *The Phenomenon of Man*, but at the same time the bare bones of his argument in that book were stated in shorter and more lucid essays. It is worthwhile to focus our attention on two short pieces that Teilhard wrote in 1945, just before and just after the end of the Second World War, during his last year in China. The first is entitled "Life and the Planets," with the subtitle "What Is Happening at This Moment on Earth?"; the second, "A Great Event Foreshadowed: The Planetization of Mankind" (*The Future of Man*, chapters VI and VII). In these essays he lays out his basic interpretation of current events, even as he characteristically stuns his reader by mentioning in the same breath events as close as the war and as remote as the origin of the planets.

In these essays, it is clear in what sense Teilhard's lifelong work was basically a work of studying man. As metaphysical as Teilhard might become at times, as much as he might emphasize the cosmic dimensions of reality, as concerned as he was to unveil the presence of God in every atom of the universe and in every minute of the day—his work is ultimately centered on man. As he says in his masterwork, however, he is dealing with the *"whole* phenomenon of man," which includes the universe and God and eternity, because man can be interpreted satisfactorily only on a scale that is large enough to include all of these dimensions.

"What is happening at this moment on earth?" This is the question that stands uppermost in Teilhard's mind. And his first response is, "That all depends on what the observer believes is the proper angle of vision on this present moment." A platitude, but it is the first step toward the goal that lies at the end of Teilhard's breathtaking train of thought. If we perceive this moment on earth in terms of quantity, moving from the very large to the very small, or vice versa, this moment on earth is insignificant. Quantitatively perceived, the stars are the primary unit in the universe. They exist in great number and diversity. Stars cluster into galaxies, which Teilhard speaks of as a "gas of stars." Galaxies, however, number millions themselves—"a gas of galaxies on top of a gas of stars." Planets are secondary phenomena in the universe when contrasted to the stars, later in time of origin, formed by chance by the purely fortuitous near contact of two stars. Planets have "no place in the normal and orthodox evolution of astral matter"; they are incidental, with perhaps one star in a million possessing them. When this incidental character of planets is considered together with the even more incidental occurrence of life on the planets, "we can see what a fantastically small figure, quantitatively speaking, our Earth cuts in the Universe." The conclusion to be drawn is the pessimistic one that James Jeans, the British astronomer, drew: that our life on earth is incidental to a universe that is indifferent and even hostile to it. Such a conclusion, however,

is so much at variance, physically, with the existence and exercise of our intelligence . . . that it cannot be the last word of Science. Following the physicists and astronomers we have thus far been contemplating the Universe in terms of the Immense—immensity of space, time, energy and number. But is it not possible that we have been looking through the wrong end of the telescope, or seeing things in the wrong light? (FM, 104).

The other end of the telescope which Teilhard chooses to look through is the category of complexity, as an alternative to quantity. Complexity is the quality a thing possesses by virtue of its being composed, first of all, of "a larger number of elements" which are, secondly, "more tightly organized among themselves." Complexity is not a matter of "*simple* multiplicity but of organized multiplicity; not simple complication but *centrated* complication." From this angle, an atom is more complex than an electron, a molecule more complex than an atom, and a living cell more complex than the chemical nuclei which

[31]

comprise it. From this angle, it is not the Earth, Sun, or stars that are the key units of reality, because they are simply aggregates, lacking organization and centeredness (or "centricity") when compared to the atom, molecule, cell, and living being.

If the physical universe is classified on the scale of complexity, we come to a quite different answer to the question, "What is happening at this moment on earth?" because it is on the planets, not on the stars, that the future of evolution lies—for the simple reason that

> it is only on the very humble planets, on them alone, that the mysterious ascent of the world into the sphere of high complexity has a chance to take place . . . it is through them that the axis of Life now passes; it is upon them that the energies of an Evolution principally concerned with the building of large molecules is now concentrated (FM, 109).

The rarity of planets and life impresses us, not with the chance character of life but with the difficulty that attends the process of complexification. Once this axiom is laid down, it is but a short step to the conclusion that life in general and man in particular are the axes of significant happenings in the universe. As one proceeds to observe the life process, it seems that greater complexity implies greater centeredness and thus greater awareness and, finally, consciousness. In *The Phenomenon of Man,* he designates this movement toward complexity and consciousness the Ariadne's Thread which constitutes the *direction* of evolution. Man then appears to occupy "a place of his own at the head of all the other 'very great complexes' evolved on Earth" (FM, 112). From this perspective, the Earth bears the fortunes of the universe, while man "bears the fortunes of the Earth." Man is the "ultra-complex" creature, because he is possessed of *self*-consciousness, which is the most intense level of complexity yet to appear.

Matter itself has reached its greatest centeredness and complexity in man. But what is happening *at this moment* on earth? If earth and its life, and man as the highest product of that life, is the axis of significant development, has this axis reached its acme? If so, what then? Teilhard reiterates one of his most persisting themes in the assertion that "No proof exists that man has come to the end of his potentialities, that he has reached his highest point" (FM, 113). What we are witnessing at this very moment on earth is the continuing development of life in man, "a peculiarly critical phase of super-humanization."

This is what I hope to persuade you of by drawing your attention to an altogether extraordinary and highly suggestive condition of the world around us, one which we all see and are subject to, but without paying any attention to it, or at least without understanding it: I mean the increasingly rapid growth in the human world of the forces of collectivization (FM, 113).

The trends toward collectivization are the latest manifestations of the organization and growing centeredness of life, the latest phase of complexification. Collectivization is the process by which an incessant multiplication of people over the spherical shape of the globe moves toward intense superorganization. This intensity of organization continues the trend toward the complexity that life has always needed in order to achieve breakthroughs into new phases of development. It will bring a heightened awareness or consciousness that will enable a new phase of evolution.

What is happening at this moment on earth? The process of complexification is passing through a new, critical phase, the phase of "socialization of Mankind." *"In our time, Mankind seems to be approaching its critical point of social organization"* (FM, 39). This superorganization, socialization, or complexification—all favorite terms in Teilhard's new dictionary—is also the era of man's *planetization.*

The present moment of the socialization or planetization of mankind is placed within an even larger train of thought in Teilhard's other writings. The basic unit with which Teilhard works is *matter,* beginning with the subatomic particles of which it is composed. This matter possesses the fundamental characteristic of tending toward ever greater complexity. When matter reaches a certain level of complexity, we call it *life,* which is characterized by growth, nutrition, and reproductive capabilities and, above all, increasing consciousness. Before reaching the phase of complexity called life, the world exists as the sphere Teilhard calls the *geosphere;* when life appears, the world moves forward into the zone of the *biosphere.* The vitalization of matter is life, but vitalization moves on into *hominization (homo =* man), and it is the characteristic of hominized matter, matter that is humanified, to become socialized and enter thus into the zone of the *noosphere (nous =* reason). The noosphere is the zone which can be described, as Teilhard does, as the "thinking envelope" or "thinking membrane" that covers the geospheric-biospheric reality of the world.

When we reflect upon living molecules, we do not think of individual molecules of matter that became vitalized, as if individual molecules were passing from inorganic to organic states. Rather, an entire zone of the physical world has become alive; life has appeared in the physical realm; we must now include as one of the conditions or states of the physical realm its vitalized state or zone. Similarly, when we think of man, we think of the appearance of man on the face of the earth, not of individual nonhuman forms giving rise to man. We think, Teilhard seems to assume, that the physical realm has added a new layer, a new state, the hominized state. A thinking membrane is now stretched over the geosphere. If this is true, then we should not think of individual human beings, either in a static phase of their development or in the process of developing into higher forms. Rather, we should conceive of humankind as a whole developing into a new form, which is at the same time a new state or condition of the physical world, of matter. This new state is the zone of the noosphere, a new layer which the physical realm has added to itself. We will have to return to a more detailed discussion of these concepts later in this chapter. It is important to see at this point, however, that within Teilhard's train of thinking, the present moment—that is, the period from about 1920 until his death in 1955 (and specifically the year 1945 at the time he was writing the two essays we have been concentrating on)—is the moment in which hominized matter enters into its next phase of planetization or socialization, a phase which is essential to building up the noosphere, that phase of the world's development which follows upon the development of geosphere and biosphere.

The remaining portions of this chapter must be devoted to unraveling the threads of argumentation by which Teilhard supports his interpretation of the events through which he was living. In order to begin the unraveling, however, we must recognize clearly the crucial step which permitted Teilhard to enter upon this entire enterprise of interpreting events as he did. I call this step Teilhard's first major extrapolation (companion to the second major extrapolation discussed in the next chapter). Teilhard spells out this extrapolation in another essay that is collected in *The Future of Man,* a 1947 piece entitled, "Turmoil or Genesis?" with the subtitle, "The Position of Man in Nature and the Significance of Human Socialization." It is of central importance for us to grasp clearly the nature of this extrapolation, for it underlies Teilhard's entire work.

In this essay, of about the same time as the other two we have analyzed, Teilhard lays down the postulate that since matter moves along the path of complexification that eventually involves consciousness (since consciousness is the quality that emerges, naturally, when a certain level of complexity is reached) and ultimately becomes self-conscious—that is, aware of itself—*it must at some time become aware of the direction and goal of its own development.* Therefore, when consciousness emerges to the point where it is perceptible, one can measure its advancing development and extrapolate from there its past and its future. He writes that

> it is the nature of Matter, when raised corpuscularly to a very high degree of complexity, to become centrated and interiorized—that is to say, to endow itself with Consciousness. *This means that the degree of consciousness attained by living creatures* (from the moment, naturally, when it becomes discernible) *may be used as a parameter to estimate the direction and speed of Evolution . . .* in terms of absolute values (FM, 218, italics added).

This represents, to my mind, a major scientific thesis which must be scrutinized carefully by the appropriate specialized sciences—not in this work, or by this writer at this time—because it is not only a fascinating thesis but central to Teilhard's method of argumentation.[1] As I understand it, to repeat, he is suggesting that consciousness in living things—culminating in man—can be taken as the touchstone or standard of measurement for all of reality, in terms of which the previous history of the world can be projected forward. Teilhard has selected one segment in the evolution of life—from the first perceptible manifestation of consciousness in subhuman organisms up to the stage of the fully developed human consciousness (which is self-consciousness)—and he has made the trends that are evident in this one segment his clue to understanding the trends that are basic to all of evolution and human history. Much of one's judgment as to the adequacy or inadequacy of his system of thought depends on a judgment concerning the validity of Teilhard's selecting this particular base for his projections. Here we should note that the warrants for Teilhard's selectivity are subjective. He *assumes* that the segment of evolutionary development he has selected is of highest significance. He assumes, in other words, that the segment that culminates in man is determinative for all the rest. This assumption is what makes his end of the telescope different from the end through which the astronomers and physicists look.

This means, as we have seen in Teilhard's answer to the question "What is happening at this moment on earth?", that the past is the history of matter—relatively simple, less complex, which is not discernibly conscious or aware—becoming more complex and conscious. The future, on the other hand, is projected as the development of ever more complexity, organization, and consciousness entering into a new phase of evolution. Teilhard reacted against a method that was too greatly bound to the physicist and astronomer in that it used the stars or subatomic particles as the touchstone, with the result that human life was both a fortuitous product of chance and of questionable significance. Rather he chose man as his touchstone, with the result that both stars and subatomic particles gain their significance by virtue of their participation in the process of complexity that produced consciousness and man. If the physicist and astronomer were allowed to dominate, then the question of what is happening at this moment on earth would be so insignificant as to be unworthy of the effort of asking it.

> Every new war, embarked upon by the nations for the purpose of detaching themselves from one another, merely results in their being bound and mingled together in a more inextricable knot. The more we seek to thrust each other away, the more do we interpenetrate (FM, 127).

The Second World War, more specifically, involved a series of events by which "since 1939 a vast expanse of the earth, the region of the Pacific, hitherto on the fringe of civilization, has for practical purposes entered irrevocably into the orbit of industrialized nations" (FM, 126). The rise of technology and cybernetics fits into Teilhard's interpretation. Mankind is becoming a "brain of brains," or "super-Brain," a "stupendous thinking machine." Teilhard did not mean to imply the intellectualistic connotations that the words "brain" and "thinking machine" might carry for us. Rather, he was referring to the total reflective activity of man, which includes self-awareness, intellectual activity, and search for meaning. This was not a cerebral flight from material things but rather a phase of the development of the material into the extremely complex. He recognized that employment patterns would be altered in the new unified state of man, leaving more leisure for some, which could not be turned back, because the role of manual labor was plainly and irrevocably changing.

This movement toward unification is central to Teilhard's thinking, representing as it does a dimension of his near obsession for unity and synthesis. It is impossible to overemphasize its centrality in his vision. Unification of mankind is the human manifestation of *convergence*, which is another of the key words in his revised dictionary. Convergence includes not only unification but also the increase in centeredness that leads to ascent up the evolutionary scale. Convergence of the human species within the noosphere is the most important step before the convergence that leads to point Omega, the final consummation (see the next chapter for a fuller discussion). Teilhard summarized this double thrust toward unification and ascent in his aphorism—which the writer Flannery O'Connor took as the title of one of her works—"Everything that rises must converge."

Collectivization and Personalization. Teilhard believed that the concept of complexity threw light on one of the most perplexing aspects of mankind's thrust toward unification, the problem of the individual over against the whole, or collectivity. As we noted earlier, Teilhard defined complexity as involving both multiplicity *and* organization, complication *and* centeredness. In terms of the movement of historical events during his lifetime, the unification or socialization of mankind was caught up in the double rhythm of collectivization and personalization. The fascist and totalitarian movements of the day were abhorrent to Teilhard (although it is true that he at times admired their organization), but he believed that they were a manifestation, even if distorted, of the necessary and healthy thrust toward unity in multiplicity. The individualistic protest against fascism was a manifestation—also distorted, in Teilhard's view—of the necessary tendency toward centeredness or personalization. It is a favorite pastime of some to accuse Teilhard of leaning toward totalitarian political views, but he reiterates many times that personality dare not be lost in the rush toward unification. Time and again he explained that true healthy union does not destroy the individual. Rather, "union differentiates." This, he believed, could be documented by a study of cell growth in an organism, as well as by observing closely the life of human groups or love between two persons. In response to a UNESCO questionnaire in 1949, he put the matter very clearly:

> Of all the structural tendencies inherent in the human mass the most fundamental (indeed, the one from which all others are derived) is undoubtedly that which has led Mankind, under the twofold influence of planetary compression and psychic interpenetration, to enter upon an irresistible process of unification and organization upon itself. But to this a vital condition is attached, namely, that if it is to be viable and stable the resulting unification must not stifle but on the contrary must exalt the incommunicable

uniqueness of each separate element in the system: something that is proved possible on a small scale by every successful team or association (FM, 239).

B. The First Extrapolation as a Key to Understanding Our Age

Teilhard proceeded very methodically, on the basis of what he thought was empirical evidence, to develop a series of categories that suggest the general significance of current history. As we have just observed, this method is that of an extrapolation or projection backward of the past history of the world and forward of its future history—an extrapolation on the basis of the perceptible development of consciousness from its smallest glimmerings in lower forms of organic life to its highest manifestations in human beings. As such this extrapolation is radically focused on man as the clue to the entire process. This extrapolation is a hypothesis, or model, of the increasing complexity of matter, calling attention to its transformation from inorganic to organic to life and hominization. Teilhard designates this extrapolation by the term *complexification*. Parenthetically, we note that here we have an example of how synthetic Teilhard's vision is, and how difficult it is to separate his science from his metaphysics and religion. He writes in the midst of his argument:

> Despite appearances and a certain overlapping due to the vastness of the subject (as we draw near to the Whole, physics, metaphysics and religion strangely converge) I am prepared to maintain that what I have to say does not anywhere go beyond the field of scientific observation. What this essay claims to offer is not philosophical speculation but an extension of our biological perspective—no more, and no less (FM, 126).

To which we can only add—Yes, if being "scientific" means selecting a specific set of data (the development of consciousness) and extrapolating from it on a vast scale. But such "science," while it may be methodical, is also philosophy and undeniably speculative! Even though it may be speculation that is consistent with the biological perspective, it is not simply "science." This may be one of the points where we can see the significance of the suggestion that Teilhard is a metaphysician in the "inductive" or "descriptive" sense that Whitehead speaks of. He obviously speculates, but his speculation takes off from a category that is *empirically* derived.

[38]

the raw power of the sense of the species, which turns the screw in order to actualize the socialization that is necessary, regardless of the individual entities and their personal identities. The totalitarian regimes represent this phase, and so do the Marxists. The enforced phase must give way to the *free* stage of development, however, because the impersonal, relentless turn of the screw cannot consummate the destiny of man; "nothing seems finally capable of guiding us into the natural sphere of our inter-human affinities except the emergence of a powerful field of internal attraction, in which we shall find ourselves caught *from within*" (FM, 287). And this internal attraction is the collectivization that moves by the power of "sympathy" or love and thus synthesizes collectivizing and personalizing trends.

Socialization must bring with it "an enhancement of [the] 'centric' qualities" (FM, 234) of the individual elements of society, and these centric qualities are synonymous with personality. Totalitarian developments in the first half of this century reveal that under

> purely enforced conditions the center of consciousness cannot achieve its natural growth . . . only union *through* love and *in* love (using the word "love" in its widest and most real sense of "mutual internal affinity"), because it brings individuals together, not superficially and tangentially but center to center, can physically possess the property of not merely differentiating but also personalizing the elements which comprise it (FM, 235).

What is happening at this moment on Earth? The rise of mass culture? Collectivization? East-West tensions? Antagonism between the state and the individual? Yes, and much more. But what does it all mean? Teilhard thought he knew, because he could interpret it all by means of his concept of complexification. This category revealed to him that the rise of collectivities was essentially to be welcomed, because it was the species actualizing its intrinsic nature. With that observation, Teilhard put current events onto the vast canvas of cosmic evolutionary history, from the beginning of the universe, and of the evolution of this planet and life. But the category of complexification was also an analysis of the more detailed mechanisms of man's collectivization, and this detailed analysis revealed why the destiny of the species could not come easily and unambiguously, because the tensions between the group and the individual, between the collective and the personal, had to be resolved in an adequate synthesis.

To Accept or Resist Mankind's Unification. Much of Teilhard's literary effort was a polemic against those who would not join him in embracing the trend toward unification. He spoke of these persons as the "immobilists," those who will not accept progress. He described, in 1920, the spectacle of

> Mankind divided to its very depths into two irrevocably opposed camps—one looking towards the horizon and proclaiming with all its new-found faith, "We are moving," and the other, without shifting its position, obstinately maintaining, "Nothing changes. We are not moving at all" (FM, 11).

These immobilists are not simply afflicted with the malaise that comes from an exclusive commitment to the status quo. Some of them are those who claim the intellectual evidence that the evolution of man is slowing down, coming to a halt, as indicated by the relative stability of his physical body. Teilhard agrees that, as an individual, there is perhaps little or no evolutionary change going on in man's body, but *as a species* man is passing through a critical moment of change, the phase of socialization, with all of the attendant alterations we have been analyzing in the preceding pages.

The opposition of these immobilists, together with those who less intentionally block mankind's development by their misuse of natural resources, their failure to heed the dangers of overpopulation, and the like, raises an important consideration for Teilhard's view of contemporary history. That question has to do with whether the process of history that he outlines happens inexorably, despite man's intentions and achievements, or whether it can be thwarted. This question will be dealt with in detail in Chapter IV, but here it is enough to observe that Teilhard expressed great confidence that the "sense of the species" would not be stymied—even though he argued that men should decide for the current trends toward socialization as if everything depended on their cooperation with the movement of history. Whether men can derail the movement of history or not, Teilhard knew that history would be, in part, the story of the conflict between those, on the one hand, who discerned the meaning of the events through which they were living in the first half of the twentieth century and therefore shaped their actions to support and advance the movement toward complexification and those, on the other hand, who either intentionally or blindly obstructed its progress toward its goal. He interpreted a great deal of the opposition to his own writings as a manifestation, within ecclesiastical circles, of the immobilist position.

Teilhard has been accused, with some justification, of being elitist in his view, conditioned by the patrician milieu in which he grew up. Nevertheless, it is remarkable how free he was from his upbringing and cultural conditionedness. In the period between the world wars he was facing the same phenomenon of mass culture which so many of his fellow patricians abhorred and condemned as barbaric. He saw its ambiguities, but his view of current events did not see the rise of mass culture as a degradation which marked the decline of the West. Rather, he saw it as the harbinger, imperfect though it might be, of a new Mankind. This rise of the masses, despite the ugly faces of fascism and the vulgarizing of culture, was in a very real sense the wave of the future, because it was essential to the collectivizing movement which was a powerful engine of mankind's thrust toward unity. Teilhard did not hesitate to point that out to the fellow members of the international elite in which he moved.

C. Basic Assumptions on Which the First Extrapolation Rests

The discussion that we have just concluded is a vast simplifying of the interpretive apparatus which Teilhard used to make sense of the events through which he lived. Now that we have his basic categories in hand, we should backtrack a bit to consider some of the most important assumptions for his thinking. Here again, however, we can select only a few of the myriad concepts he employed, and our perspective subsumes all of Teilhard's concepts under his attempt to give meaning to contemporary history through his concept of complexification.

Phenomenology—A Global and Synthetic Science. Claude Cuénot, Teilhard's biographer, speaks of Teilhard's long-time personal goal to establish an ideal scientific enterprise which he terms "a global and synthetic science." This science would proceed on the assumption that there are organic connections among all living things and that this organic network of living things is intrinsically related to the inorganic, physico-chemical, system of the earth, which is in turn set within the cosmic processes of the universe.[2] Cuénot quotes a 1933 letter of Teilhard's in which he talks about constructing a "phenomenology" which would satisfy the demand for wholeness that underlies all scientific compartmentalization by putting together "a continuous series of *phenomena* extending . . . from the spiritual to the material pole of experience."[3] A letter dated three years later speaks of utilizing the methods of science to create "an ultraphysics" which would displace the "metaphysics of which we are dying." This "ultraphysics" would be a science in which "matter and spirit would be embraced in one single coherent and homogeneous explanation of the world."[4]

This global science certainly figured in the definition of the categories we have discussed, in terms of which Teilhard interpreted current events. The ramifications of this phenomenology are set forth in a marvelously lucid introduction he wrote in 1943 for *Geobiologia,* a journal (which lived for only two issues!) of the Institute of Geobiology that Teilhard and his friends established in China as an umbrella organization to coordinate their studies of the geology and the flora and fauna of the Asiatic continent. The following long quotation suggests what Teilhard was after. He points to a growing body of evidence,

contributed by scientists of all disciplines, showing that;
First, the world of life, taken as a whole, forms a single system bound to the surface of the earth; a system whose elements, in whatever order of association they may be considered, are not simply thrown together and molded upon one another like grains of sand, but are organically interdependent like the pipelines of a hydrodynamic system, or like molecules caught in a capillary surface.

Secondly, this organic sheet, which is spread over the whole surface of what is often called the "crust" but is in fact chemically the most active "sphere" of our planet, is not, either in its genesis or in its duration, physically separable from the general mass of the earth it covers. The earth is not merely a spatial support for, but the very matrix of, this living envelope. Hence the growing importance science attaches to the notion of the *biosphere,* considering it not as a mere metaphoric entity but as a physical reality, as objective and as essential to the earth as the various other "spheres" (mineral, liquid, gaseous) whose concentric structure constitutes our planet.

The notion that the inorganic matter of the earth constitutes a natural whole whose elements . . . manifest in their proportions and arrangement a definite structure and composition bound up with the atomic and sidereal architecture of the universe, is one long since accepted by chemists and physicists . . . And now the same current of thought manifests itself in the domain of *life*, leading to the same results . . .

We already have geophysics and geochemistry. Now, completing the triad, appears geobiology . . . The study first of all of the organic links of every description that are recognizable between living beings considered in their *totality as a single closed system*. And, secondly, the study of the physico-chemical links by which the birth and development of this living envelope are bound up with the history of the planet.[5]

Teilhard is really setting forth, in other words, a view which looks upon human life and the movement of mankind in the present age as the latest phase of the cosmic and geological process that formed the universe and our planet. As he indicates elsewhere, anthropology is concerned with the latest phase of geology; or, geology is preparatory to the study of history!

The category of complexification, with its twofold thrust of multiplicity and centeredness or organization, is the link that binds all of the spheres of reality together. Life is thus defined as "vitalized matter," as matter in a higher form of complexity, and consciousness is matter in an extraordinary state of complexity. "Spirit" is thus not set in antithesis to matter but is rather within the material continuum, at a very much advanced stage of complexification.

Within the framework of the image suggested by this "ultraphysical" view of reality, we can understand more clearly Teilhard's concepts of the geosphere, the biosphere, and the noosphere. They refer to the successive "spheres" or "envelopes" which, put together, comprise the reality of this planet and the continuum of the evolutionary development of matter and life. When Teilhard speaks of the hominization of matter, he means, quite literally, that the stuff of the world, which has assumed different forms and assumed various stages of development in the formation of the earth and its flora and fauna, has attained a new stage that we call man, or humanified matter.

Teilhard's suggestions concerning his phenomenology, which is a unified global science, manifest very clearly his tremendous desire for *synthesis*. Philosophically, he must be classified as a monist, in that he exhibited an irresistible concern for unity that seemed hardly capable of tolerating any conceptuality that entertained the notion that reality was ultimately diverse or fragmented. This frame of mind, when implemented by means of the synthetic scientific method set forth here, led Teilhard to move back and forth between biology and sociology and history in a way that is staggering to the mind. His theory of complexi-fication makes the leap from the study of lower forms of life to the study of man and his society with great ease. Is this legitimate? Can we generalize so easily, subsuming both fruit flies and rats, on the one hand, and man and societies, on the other, under the same universal categories of interpretation? Teilhard recognized that there are method-ological difficulties in such a venture, but he was nevertheless convinced that they could be overcome, because the organic approach was, in his opinion, common to both biology and sociology. He believed that the work of the great sociologists, Comte, Durkheim, and others, demon-strated that "Mankind has come to present itself to our gaze . . . as a biological entity" (FM, 155).

It is in this context that Teilhard gives his detailed analyses of his concept of the noosphere. The noosphere is a biological entity, in that it is a phase of man's growth and development that stands in continuity with previous development. Within a three-year period, from January, 1947, through October, 1949, Teilhard published three highly impor-tant articles in *Revue des Questions Scientifiques* (*The Future of Man*, chapters X, XIII, XVII) detailing the concept of the noosphere. The noosphere appears in these essays as the phase of development that becomes possible only after life has already reached the stage of com-plexity that we call consciousness. The noosphere is an increased level of complexity, which in this case means an increase in centeredness (or centration), which is Teilhard's way of referring to the mechanism by which consciousness is increased, raised to a higher level, by turning in upon itself to become the self-consciousness of the species. Individual human beings have already attained self-awareness, but the noosphere is the milieu that comes into being when the species itself, as species, attains self-awareness. The events of world history during the first half of this century, which Teilhard called socialization, were in fact manifestations of this growing species self-consciousness.

Here we can see how difficult it is to assess Teilhard's thought and language. The concept of a process of increasing complexity is perhaps fairly clear. But how does one describe that process when it involves the emergence of the self-awareness of the species? Teilhard employs such elusive metaphors as "turning in upon itself"—when the human self-awareness manifested in the species becomes aware of itself, it turns inward in an intensified centeredness. "Rebound" of consciousness refers to the same process, as do the evocative images of "coiling in upon itself" and "cosmic recoil." The process is both "reflection" and "reflexion," in that it refers to both the reflective activity which focuses on the self and the reflexive character of that activity. These images do indeed communicate, and we feel that we have a "sense" for what Teilhard means, but he has moved out of the realm of ordinary scientific observation into the realm of metaphor and symbol—it is, after all, impossible to describe literally what the mechanism is of a consciousness coiling and recoiling! Nevertheless, Teilhard does often detail what these metaphors imply and illustrate them with concrete examples. His first essay on the noosphere discusses the concept under the headings of the "zoological structure of the noosphere," its "anatomy," its "physiology," and the phases of its growth. What it amounts to is a brilliant, evocative discussion of the human species developing into *a single, unified, self-conscious system of life.* What does such a system look like? Like a Brain of brains, a superorgan, a cybernetic system, in which computers and machines and telecommunications all play a role, as extensions of man's biological organism. One can hardly resist the guess that Marshall McLuhan has drunk deeply at Teilhard's fountain of vision, that what McLuhan has described is the history of developments within Teilhard's noosphere.

The Primacy of Evolution. Although we have not used the term extensively, our discussion of Teilhard's assumptions implies at every point that his system of thought is essentially a system premised on evolution. By using the term evolution, we point to several dimensions of meaning. Teilhard accepted, of course, without question the various forms of the scientific theory of evolution that pertained to his work in geology, paleontology, and biology, as well as the theories utilized by the astronomers in their descriptions of cosmic evolution. It would also be proper to say, however, that Teilhard utilized the evolutionary scheme of thought—perhaps even more importantly—as a total world view that has wider implications than its use as a specific hypothesis in any particular scientific investigation. As a broader world view, the evolutionary scheme made a twofold impact on Teilhard's system of thought: (1) it called attention to the primacy of change and movement, as intrinsic to man and his world, and (2) it established the principle of continuity, whereby Teilhard could conceive of all of reality existing on a continuum, reaching from inorganic matter to the highest manifestations of the human spirit—the differences between the phases of the continuum are clear, but their unity is also emphatically stressed within the one process of complexification.

This is not the place to review the theory of evolution as it functions in the various special sciences. Teilhard has been the center of controversy in respect to his scientific understanding of evolution. First of all, he has been criticized for his relative lack of acquaintance with the principles of genetics and the genetic interpretation of the mechanisms by which evolution proceeds in living organisms. This may seem to be a strange oversight in Teilhard's education, but it is apparently the case, even though the precise extent of this failing and its impact is more ambiguous; it seems to have affected the general validity of his work very little.

The much more significant issue in Teilhard's conception of evolution has to do with the argument of long standing over whether evolution follows an entirely random course or whether it is in some sense directed—and, if the latter, in what sense it is directed. Teilhard subscribes at many places in his writings to the view that evolution is directed, and he uses a term to express his views that is generally abhorred by biologists, *orthogenesis*. This has resulted in much criticism of Teilhard, since in previous periods "orthogenesis" was frequently used by theologians and philosophers as a means of introducing some divine or metaphysical "purpose" into the natural process of evolution. There have been articles even in recent years that have seriously criticized Teilhard for smuggling "purpose" into his evolutionary schemes.[6] As a number of "Teilhard watchers" have indicated, however, it is not enough to ascribe guilt to a man because of his choice of words—however unfortunate that choice might be; one must also pay close attention to the way he uses those words.[7] To summarize a complicated argument, when Teilhard uses the term "orthogenesis," he means to indicate two things.

1. Evolution is not, at all levels, entirely random; there are antichance factors built into the process, the factor of the organism's past development, which obviously inclines it toward some avenues of development rather than others, and the demands of the environment, which favor certain avenues over others. Thus, Teilhard uses the term "orthogenesis" to refer to the "drift" of development that results from each generation building upon previous forms. In this sense, evolution "gropes" its way, but it is influenced by the gropings of its predecessor stages and by its environment. Teilhard is not wholly consistent in this matter, and our interpretation may be supplying a clarity he did not, but it is clear that he believed that the "direction" or "drift" of evolution could be documented without recourse to divine revelation or special

insight. It was the drift toward complexification and the noosphere. Some scientists point out that Teilhard could have expressed himself without using the loaded terms he did, inasmuch as neo-Darwinian forms of evolutionary theory, relying on natural selection, also call attention to the antichance factors and the "groping" that Teilhard wished to emphasize.[8]

2. The role of chance in evolution is not the same after man's appearance as before. In at least three essays,[9] Teilhard makes it clear that random chance may indeed have prevailed in the evolution of life prior to man. Since then, however, man himself has taken a hand in his evolution. The rise of the noosphere is a sign that evolution has become conscious of itself, inasmuch as species self-awareness is awareness of the aims of evolution (i.e., toward increased complexification—collectivization plus personalization) and is self-conscious action toward the accomplishment of those aims.

Principles and Processes of the Theory of Complexification. If it is not already clear from the preceding remarks, we should enter into the record here that the axiom which Teilhard arrived at through his first major extrapolation was intended as a scientific conclusion of definite importance. Teilhard himself spoke of his basic thesis of complexification as the "cosmic law of complexity and consciousness," and he lays out the axiomatic character of the thesis in several places, including the essay on planetization mentioned earlier, *The Phenomenon of Man* (see the "Postscript"), and most forcefully in *Man's Place in Nature* (written in 1950, this book is a brief, exceedingly succinct summary of his masterwork).

The law of complexity/consciousness stands as the very core of Teilhard's theoretical scientific contribution to man's understanding of himself, history, and his world. Clustered around it are three supporting ideas that are essential to Teilhard's vision, which have aroused both admiration and controversy among Teilhard's readers. They are (1) the idea of the "within" of things, (2) the distinction between "radial" and "tangential" energy, and (3) the suggestion that the most fundamental tendency of the universe is anti-entropic in nature.

1. Teilhard speaks of every entity possessing both a "within" and a "without," and this pair of categories is proportional to several other pairs:

without/within
material interpretation of the world/spiritual interpretation of the world

[49]

material organization/psychic centering
collectivation/personalization

The "within" is the interior reality of an entity, and Teilhard links it to both consciousness (growth of consciousness is a heightening of the process of "interiorization") and spontaneity (or freedom). The term is Teilhard's way of asserting that everything that exists possesses consciousness or a psychic life. The "within" and the "without" are simultaneous dimensions of a thing, and, although we are ordinarily accustomed to observe only the "without," Teilhard looks forward to the day when science will be sensitive to the "within," as well.

The "within" thus serves several useful purposes in Teilhard's system of thought. Although, in inorganic objects, the level of psychic life or consciousness is so attenuated as to be imperceptible, the presence of a "within" establishes a basis of continuity with the full psychic phenomena that appear higher up in the process of complexification. Since the "within" is the potential thrust of centration which is the seat of an entity's identiy and awareness, it provides a basis for asserting that centeredness is present, at least potentially, throughout the evolutionary spectrum. The "within," in other words, is the precise locus of the mechanisms of complexification (and centeredness), and as such it is the nucleus of Teilhard's entire mode of thought. So he can write, *"Spiritual perfection (or conscious' centreity') and material synthesis (or complexity) are but the two aspects or connected parts of one and the same phenomenon"* (PM, 60f). The evolution of life is the process of complexification—that is, the process in which the "without," which appears to dominate our perception of the geosphere and even the biosphere, gives way to the dominance of the "within." The present age is really the age of the "within"—that is, the age in which the consciousness of the species, its psychic life of self-awareness, comes to be the chief movement of significance in human history—the rise of the noosphere. Early in *The Phenomenon of Man,* on page 61, after discussing the "within" and the "without," Teilhard observes that "In sum, all the rest of this essay will be nothing but the story of the struggle in the universe between the unified *multiple* and the unorganized *multitude:* the application throughout of the great *Law of complexity and consciousness.* " The struggle, or tension, between the "within" and the "without."

Teilhard thus stands with Bergson and Whitehead, among others, in his insistence on at least a potential consciousness in even inorganic entities. It is difficult at times to ascertain whether Teilhard really believed that the "within" exists as a dimension or characteristic of all things or whether this is his evocative way of saying that if there is a fundamental unity between all entities (both physical and spiritual), then the consciousness that appears at one end of the evolutionary scale must also exist at least in potentiality throughout, even at the opposite end.

2. Among the matched pairs of categories listed above that correspond to the "without" and the "within," we should place the terms "tangential" energy and "radial" energy. The discussion of these types of energy is analogous to the discussion of the "without" and the "within," both in its intention and its evocativeness and ambiguity. There have been attempts to take Teilhard literally and to locate the two energies. For example, P. B. Medawar and George Riggan suggest that radial energy may correspond to what the recent advances in information theory call "information content."[10] Such attempts, although interesting and illuminating, end in a certain confusion and conclude that Teilhard's theory of "two" energies is not empirically demonstrable. Dobzhansky, on the other hand, writes that the distinction should not be taken literally: "Now Teilhard surely does not claim to have discovered two new kinds of energy previously unkown to physicists and to physiologists."[11] Unfortunately, Dobzhansky himself is not clear in his explanation of what Teilhard means. We might conclude, analogous to our explanation of the "within," that Teilhard is speaking evocatively, not about an energy he can measure like information but rather about the obvious power that entities, particularly living things, possess to actualize complexity and centeredness, identity and awareness of that identity.

Such an explanation makes sense of the elusive statements Teilhard does make about radical and tangential energy:

> We shall assume that, essentially, all energy is psychic in nature [because all energy ultimately moves toward the evolution of the noosphere?]; but add that in each particular element this fundamental energy is divided into two components: a *tangential energy* which links the element with all others of the same order (that is to say, of the same complexity and the same centricity) as itself in the universe; and a *radial energy* which draws it towards ever greater complexity and centricity—in other words forwards. In this view, . . . tangential energy represents "energy" as such, as generally understood by science (PM, 64f).

Teilhard posits the two energies as constructs to make sense of what he admits is "one of the most difficult of all things": to understand how the "within" and the "without" are related to each other—that is, how simple multiplicity or aggregation is related to the process of centeredness, how the drive toward centeredness, identity, and self-awareness is both dependent upon and independent of material forces (PM, 63). Radial energy is the construct he posits to explain how centerdness is able to actualize itself. Radial energy is described in terms reminiscent of those Teilhard used in his 1948 essay on the love that is necessary to move out of the enforced collectivization of the totalitarian state into the free growth of unity which "brings individuals together, not superficially and tangentially but center to center," as we spoke of this above (FM, 235).

The assertion of the "within" of things and of "radial" energy points to a construct that Teilhard had to posit, because, even though they cannot be located empirically, it *is* empirically obvious that the thrust toward centeredness and the highest self-consciousness of the total human species is the most significant event of our time (at least Teilhard thought so). If this be so, the capacity or potentiality for that centeredness must be intrinsic to all matter (the "within"), even if it is so attenuated as to be imperceptible in lower forms. Further, that potential must be capable of actualization, therefore implying that the motive force or energy to accomplish the actualization must be real (radial energy). In this way, the intricate and almost baffling Teilhardian concepts of "within" and "radial" energy can be seen to be fundamental metaphysical assumptions on which the interpretation of contemporary history under the rubric of complexification rests. But they are metaphysical in the descriptive, inductive mode that Whitehead and Barbour speak of.

3. We can only mention here one of the most fascinating implications that derive from Teilhard's theory of complexification; it is much too technical to be dealt with in any detail. One of the basic axioms accepted by scientists is the so-called "Second Law of Thermodynamics," which has to do with the continual decline in the amount of energy that exists to perform work in any given "system" or context. The tendency for energy to decline is termed "entropy," and the ultimate result of a decline in energy is a state of equilibrium in which no work is done at all, but rather the system is in a state of rest.[12] Since our solar system, our planet, and the evolutionary process of life on Earth itself all qualify as closed systems, the conclusion is drawn that

the energy supply available to us is finite; it cannot last forever, but on the contrary it will surely decline. Teilhard's theory of complexification suggests that the Second Law of Thermodynamics is neutralized by a counter principle, that anti-entropic forces are most basic, since their energies sustain the ever-increasing centration and complexification that enhance our self-consciousness and enable mankind's unification. In *Man's Place in Nature,* Teilhard bluntly offers the theory of complexification as a counterweight, or at least a parallel, to the theory of entropy and the Second Law of Thermodynamics (MPN, 33 f.; also PM, 217 f.). Since he believed that man naturally is destined to attain higher forms of centeredness, Teilhard was compelled to assert that the energy to achieve those forms must be present, and therefore entropy cannot be the final word.

D. Getting Our Bearings

Perhaps the most pressing problem that confronts the reader after he has once surveyed Teilhard's basic interpretation of events is the dual one of its vastness and its strangeness. What does it all mean? Leaping from the cosmic process of planet formation to the Second World War—is it more than simple fantasy? And the manufactured terms, "complexification," "centricity," "noosphere"—do they refer to anything real, or are they simply confusion? I would suggest that Teilhard's interpretation of contemporary events is clarified greatly when we recognize that, stripped to its barest outlines, it points to a fundamental trend which he believed is dominating man's development: that the human population of the planet Earth has reached the point in its history when it recognizes that its destiny is moving it toward the formation of *a single unified system encompassing the entire planet.* To the description of this trend he adds two important assertions about man's development: first, that this single unified system will be of *a type appropriate to the level of development man has attained as the most complex, self-conscious creature yet to appear;* second, that this present moment in the history of man holds *a consistent place in the evolution of the Earth and the living forms that exist upon it.* If we keep in mind this fundamental trend toward system formation and the two qualifying assertions that describe it, we can visualize the basic unity of Teilhard's thought and thereby understand what his analysis and its accompanying terminology intend to accomplish.

When Teilhard speaks of "planetization," "socialization," "convergence," and the like, he is pointing to that movement toward the unified, planet-encompassing system. What we must keep in mind is that Teilhard devotes an enormous amount of effort to describe this system within the terms that are set up by the two qualifying assertions we referred to—namely (1) the *appropriateness* of the system to man's level of being and (2) the *relationship* of the system and its development to the total history of the planet and its life.

1. What type of a unified system is appropriate to man? Or, to put it in another way, If human society is forming of itself a single vast system, what kind of a system will it be? Teilhard says that it will be a system which is self-conscious about itself and which embodies the psychic and personality values of human life—inasmuch as man is, when compared with other creatures, above all distinguished by his *self-*consciousness and his psychic development toward integrated personality. A system comprised of human beings could hardly be less than fully self-conscious, since man is a self-aware creature. This is what Teilhard is after in his concern for species awareness, the "sense of the species," the "sense of evolution." Men have long been aware of themselves as individuals, but the critical phase of our history that is marked by the twentieth century is that the species, mankind, is developing full awareness *as a species.* In non-Teilhardian jargon, this implies that all of mankind, the entire planet over, is becoming one vast *cybernetically functioning system.* A cybernetically functioning system is one which forms the kind of unity that is able to visualize its objectives and all of the internal and external factors that affect the accomplishment of those objectives, and which is able *to alter its behavior, as a system, in light of those factors.* Cybernetically functioning systems operate according to what are called *servo-mechanisms*—that is, mechanisms that not only do the work they have to do but which also measure their progress toward accomplishing that work through "feedback" and alter their functioning accordingly, so that the work can be achieved in the light of external and internal factors that might hinder or otherwise affect that achievement. All living organisms are cybernetically functioning systems, and we have built many mechanical systems that operate similarly. The heating system in a house is a simple cybernetically functioning system. It gets the work done that is necessary to heat our homes. If a blizzard lowers the temperature outside to zero, the system can detect the consequences of that temperature drop, feed that information back into its operation, alter its functioning, pour out

more heat for a longer time, and still maintain 72 degrees of heat inside. If a balmy season sets in, the heating system can also react accordingly. When Teilhard speaks of the formation of the noosphere and its distinctive character, he is calling attention to the quantative and qualitative differences that apply to a planet-encompassing system that is formed by thinking, self-conscious, personal creatures—that is, by human beings. These differences have to do with the vastly more complex relationships that man can enter into, relationships that are not simply physical but which are intellectual, spiritual or psychic, personality-centered. When Teilhard speaks of this planetary human system as a "Brain of brains," he is underscoring these differences. Chief among them is self-consciousness, since total awareness is necessary if the feedback necessary to the system of mankind is to develop.

Teilhard's emphasis on the preservation and enhancement of the personal identity of the individual human beings that comprise the planetary system is clear from his repeated insistence that collectivization must go hand in hand with *personalization. Centeredness* as a person also belongs to this same concern. Personalization is one of the internal considerations that the self-conscious system must take into account as it grows and functions. When Teilhard applauds the legitimate collective concern of totalitarianism and the legitimate personal concern of democracy, and yet criticizes both of them for their inadequate attention to the total needs of collectivity *and* personality, he is really saying that totalitarianism and democracy are two useful and necessary attempts that nevertheless fall short of providing the most adequate model for the political and social form of the planetary human system. The most adequate model will incorporate the legitimate thrusts of both, but it will overcome the onesidedness of each. It will embody *both* the collective *and* the personal.

2. Teilhard's second primary assertion holds that the formation of the planetary human system does not take place in isolation, but rather fits consistently into the total evolutionary development of the world and life. Teilhard's concern for a synthetic phenomenology or global science calls attention to this relatedness between the formation of the human system and the evolutionary phases that have gone before. His very notions of "complexification" and the "within/without" and "radial/tangential" distinctions carry with them the indicators that reveal the bonds between what is happening in human development and what has happened before in the development of predecessor systems on Earth.

[55]

It is clear now why Teilhard is so concerned to look through the end of the telescope that focuses on complexity rather than the end that sees only the immense and the infinitesimal. Only by focusing on man and his consciousness as he does and by making his first significant extrapolation concerning complexification is it possible to (1) see the importance of what is happening "at this moment on earth" and (2) relate it to the total evolutionary process. If man is not central in that focus, and if complexity is not the key for interpreting events, then one of two things will result: *either* one will focus on the evolutionary process, as the astronomer and the physicist do, and will conclude as James Jeans did that man is a fortuitous manifestation in a hostile universe; *or* one will focus on man and correctly sense the importance of the present era, but will be unable to relate human history to the entire scheme of things, with man thus being considered a perplexing anomaly.

Now if the promise of Teilhard's life and thought lies primarily in the judgment he made concerning the significance of the first half of the twentieth century, we must subject that judgment to scrutiny. The next chapters will suggest that a great many other issues spin off of this primary judgment, but for the moment we must focus on it. The idea that mankind is becoming one is certainly not a new one, and Teilhard is simply one of many who have proclaimed the gospel of "one world" and the "global village." But what can we say about Teilhard's specific version of this gospel—humankind as a planetary system, functioning cybernetically, emphasizing the self-consciousness of the system, its concern for individual integrity, and its relationship to the geophysical and biological support systems that preceded it in the evolutionary process and continue to coexist with it?

As these pages were being written, the Apollo moon exploration project successfully completed its landing of men on the Moon. It is tempting to place that entire project within the Teilhardian framework. The Apollo 9 mission of circling the Moon brought with it an almost poignant expression of what it means for man to recognize at last that he is *a* species, localized on *a* planet, Earth. To behold the Earth from the other side of its gravitational field, whether as an astronaut or through his television pictures, brought home what it means to be a member of a total species. Despite all the propaganda ploys, the essential validity of the comments that this space venture transcends national boundaries could not be hidden. The first words of Neil Armstrong were incredibly Teilhardian—"One small step for a man, a giant leap for mankind." It *was* one man's small step, but the species consciousness that accompanied that step made it a step for all men. Hand in hand with the species consciousness and species pride that attended the Apollo 11 flight, however, came species reflection upon its significance, upon the most appropriate kind of action that the species should pursue, about the priority of values that the species should establish. Should the species first fly to Mars or rather divert money to fight poverty? The naïve "hurrahs" and the critical opposition to the space program alike manifested the planetization or species awareness that the moon landing exemplified. But they manifest differing degrees of sensitivity to the questions of value that accompany that species awareness: "What kind of system and what kind of activity are most appropriate to the human species?" "What is the best means for assuring the preservation of the individual's personal integrity within the over-all activity of the species system?" Incidentally, it is interesting to recall that Teilhard foresaw the human desire to escape Earth's problems by fleeing to other planets. He considered it unlikely that such an escape would prove feasible.

It is impossible to bring the kinds of specialized judgment to bear here that are necessary for evaluating Teilhard's judgments about contemporary history. It does seem clear, however, that his thesis concerning the emergence of a planetary and self-conscious system of humankind, operating to preserve personal integrity, is very much worth exploring, testing out, and utilizing as a key for interpreting the problems and possibilities of contemporary life. That it may be in error at points and in need of revisions does not invalidate its promise as a thesis or model for stimulating further reflection. The issues that called forth Teilhard's theories are the pressing issues that dominate thinking today wherever men search for the meaning of the events of our own history. Today, for example, we are well aware of the adequacies and inadequacies of our responses to the challenge of the future, and we are turning our attention to the question of what we must do to survive in the decades ahead. We are aware that the human species must consider itself as a global system; the national and racial and social groups within the system must behave accordingly; they must attend to the delicate ecological interrelationships that exist between human life and the natural environment. These are the issues that Teilhard considered to be pre-eminent for twentieth-century man, and the decade and a half since his death has borne out the correctness of his vision. Ecologists, urban planners, and social scientists generally seem to share a consensus in suggesting that the fundamental prerequisite for our survival is the development of a comprehensive world view that Victor Ferkiss describes as being based on three principles: (1) "the new naturalism" —"which asserts that man is part of nature rather than something apart from it"; (2) "the new holism"—"the realization of how interconnected everything is"; (3) "the new immanentism"—the awareness that the "mind-body-society-nature" totality of the world system is "determined not from outside but from within." The gist of this world view is that of a cybernetically functioning system, expressed by Ferkiss thus:

> If man and nature are one, then society and the environment are one. Therefore, meaningful social policies must be ecological in character, that is, they must be based on a recognition that the interrelationship of men to each other and to the total environment means that any decision, any change, affects everything in the total system.[13]

Planning within the system functions as a servo-mechanism, as the "self-consciousness of the human element in developing patterns of interrelation." From this world view of the "mind-body-society-nature" system, the norms which emerge in Ferkiss' strategy for the future, which he shares with such diverse current analysts as John Kenneth Galbraith, Leroy Augenstein, Michael Harrington, Theodosius Dobzhansky, Theodore Roszak, and Paul Ehrlich,[14] are very much of a piece with Teilhard's: Mankind is entering the phase of its development which marks it as a total species system, placing upon it the imperatives to be self-conscious *as a system,* to preserve personal integrity, and to recognize the interrelatedness of man and nature.

Teilhard's analysis was relentless in its emphasis upon the self-consciousness and process of personalization that must dominate within the planetary community that is driving toward system formation. These three factors still appear to be helpful rubrics under which much of the current scene can be understood more clearly. One of the impressive aspects of Teilhard's analysis is that it accounts for the tendencies toward both *unity* and *conflict* that are apparent today. This double rhythm, between harmony (unity) and conflict, has perplexed many of us. The rhythm runs through every aspect of current history. The movement toward integration of the races in the United States and also toward "black power" and separatism; the thrust toward unity among the communist states and also the nationalism that crops up behind the

Iron Curtain; the thrust toward centralization of government in our nation, under the "liberals," and the cry for decentralization from the "conservatives" and "radicals"; the "politicization" of much of contemporary society, calling for activism more intense than ever before, coexisting with the philosophy of "do your own thing" that comes from the privatized world of the middle class as well as from hippiedom. The dilemma that confronts the sensitive observer and participant is that the unifying and the separatist tendencies *both* seem to share healthy and pathological dimensions. The dilemma is that of choosing between them. Sociologists have pointed out that a great deal depends upon whether one interprets contemporary events with a bias toward *unity* or toward *conflict* as the natural and desirable state of affairs. Sociologists who adopted a conflict model foresaw the current deepening of racial antagonism in the United States, for example, whereas those who chose a harmony model did not.[15] To operate with either bias is to distort reality; to be forced to choose between them is impossible for most. Teilhard offers the outlines, at least, of an interpretation that helps to resolve this dilemma, because he indicates that both the thrust toward unity and the conflict between individuals and between groups are fundamental and permanent characteristics of reality. Collectivization is a movement toward unity that must always allow for personalization, because the self-assertion (or drive toward centeredness and identity) of individuals and groups cannot be stifled in the long run. Much of the dissent that sweeps the globe today and that permeates all aspects of social life—from nationalistic Marxist groups in Eastern Europe to women's liberation and black liberation—is intelligible as the force of personalization and centeredness that is reacting to depersonalizing and even tyrannizing collectivism in one form or another. Teilhard's categories can comprehend the dissolution of a liberal perspective which integrated blacks with little regard for their blackness, as if they were simply dark-hued white men; these categories also throw light on the inadequacy of a male orientation in society that either ignores the equality of women or espouses a feminism which defines that equality in terms of the accessibility of male values rather than in terms of the feminization of masculine-oriented structures. On the other hand, personalization cannot take place apart from the larger whole; thus, there is a check against the extreme of separatism. In 1947, Teilhard wrote an essay on peace (FM, Chapter IX). Peace will come, he writes, without question. The question, rather, is "What kind of peace?" Peace is neither "bourgeois tranquility" nor "millennary felicity." Peace is not tranquility but rather "some sort of tense cohesion pervaded and inspired with the same energies, now become harmonious, which were previously wasted in bloodshed." For this reason, he believes, pacifism will not necessarily bring peace; peace is not the elimination of warfare but rather its sublimation.

Teilhard has been criticized for his lack of attention to the psychological dimension of human existence. It is true that he was not well-informed concerning psychology, nor did he give the same extended treatment to the work of psychologists that he gave to other fields. On the other hand, his interpretation of human nature and contemporary history is impressive precisely because of the sound psychological assumptions that it reveals concerning the role of centeredness and identity in the formation of the self, the role of self-awareness, and the irrevocable rights of personal integrity—all within the context of the corporate nature of man.[16]

Teilhard's fundamental vision of the present age as the Age of Mankind's Entrance into Planetary System Formation is provocative, if it is nothing else. Even if his vision were to be in large part discarded, it proves its promise simply by the stimulus it provides for exploring a wide range of significant questions concerning the meaning of man for our time. There are, nevertheless, a number of considerations that must be kept in mind if we are to evaluate Teilhard properly. First of all, we must recognize that Teilhard is not fully original in his thinking. In many respects, he is a man whose idea had become ripe in society as a whole, and its very ripeness accounted for his popularity. He has been influenced by many other thinkers—a factor we have not even touched upon in this study. His ability, moreover, lay rather in his power to bring together a staggeringly broad range of material and synthesize it into one vision. Time and again, it is his power to synthesize that impresses us as his forte. Secondly, as we consider Teilhard's placement in the contemporary scene, we must also remember that several other thinkers have gone into much more detail than he, and more satisfactorily, with more specialized skill, in discussing certain segments of the material that he included within his synthesis. Teilhard did not function with equal competence in every area he touched upon—an occupational hazard, we might add, among great synthesizers! It is not surprising that in some areas others are more promising than he. A thinker like Teilhard, who proposes to write about everything, ends up being definitive about nothing. Whitehead, for example, and S. C. Alexander, have dealt with the "within" of things, under different rubrics, and have provided what are fuller and probably more adequate discussions of the psychism, incipient or actual, in all things, from the bottom to the top of the evolutionary scale. Similarly, when it comes to the actual, concrete process of evolutionary development, whether it pertains to subatomic particles or man, Teilhard's analysis is vague and imprecise when compared to the meticulous discussions of Whitehead and Alexander.[17] Thirdly, it is obvious that he was an amateur in his sociological and historical assessments, even though his basic interpretations are provocative. Up to this time, however, it has been chiefly the natural scientists and the theologians who have taken Teilhard seriously as pertaining to their fields. His thinking has not been subjected to the scrutiny of the social scientists, although our suggestions indicate that his concern for meaning in contemporary history places him very much within the range of the social sciences.

Much could be said about Teilhard's global phenomenology or unified scientific method. Let us simply summarize by suggesting that the motives which underlay Teilhard's effort to construct such a science are widely applauded. There are persisting efforts to break out of the confinements of the existing compartmentalized sciences and to integrate their findings. In the past year, for example, at least one important scholarly journal, entitled *The Human Context,* was founded with the aim of encouraging interdisciplinary studies of man. Interdisciplinary institutes are leapfrogging with some success over the traditional fragmenting barriers to a holistic view of man and the world. Whether Teilhard succeeded in establishing the global science he wanted is another question, however. His leaps from geology to biology to anthropology to history and sociology beggar all comparison. Only a metaphysically "free spirit" could perform the intellectual gymnastics he executes. He was aware of the dangers, however, and he explicitly cautions against hasty and naive generalizations that violate the integrity of the materials he is pulling together. But he was not able to carry through his generalizations without faltering here and there. His category of complexification as a vehicle for moving from matter to spirit and man has received favorable comment from some scientists, but "complexity" is itself not an unambiguous concept, and more evidence and corroboration need to be collected.[18] His assumption that society can be understood according to the organic model may be accepted by many, but cultural anthropologists and sociologists have developed categories and principles for understanding the evolution of the human social organism that are methodologically quite distinct from those used by biologists.[19] Here Teilhard's training in paleontology served him well, because it meant that he was never inclined to approach the evolution of life from the strictly biological point of view in isolation from anthropological categories.

Teilhard's global scientific method is, in the last analysis, guided by intuition, and it cannot claim to be a "science" in any conventional sense of that term. It would be helpful if Teilhard's defenders would accept this fact, rather than attempting to defend it as "science." Nevertheless, now that we are beginning to appreciate that intuition plays an important role in science, we know that such a verdict does not mean that Teilhard's phenomenology is contrary to science, uninformed by science, or scientifically useless. Furthermore, as Dobzhansky reminds us, Teilhard's world view was thoroughly shaped by the scientific vision. The intuition that enables him to move from geology to sociology and history is the kind of intuition we would expect from a man who was fully at home in scientific research, who was a child of a scientific age. We would go even further and say that his intuition would have been impossible for a man who was not scientifically trained.

Voices from many quarters argue, as Teilhard does, that it is urgently important for the species of man to develop the system consciousness, the "mind-body-society-nature" perspective, that Teilhard urges. A pertinent question arises, however, when we compare Teilhard with social scientists and ecologists who specialize in the study of the interrelationships between man and the natural support systems that the world provides for him. These men warn us that there is a very good possibility that the human species will *not* develop this consciousness quickly enough to avoid extinction, and therefore man will not be able to carry out the measures that are necessary for his survival. Teilhard was definitely aware of the possibility that the human species could perish through an inadequate response to the challenges of the time. Indeed, he devoted a lifetime to exhorting his fellow men to prepare themselves for the proper responses. Nevertheless, he was thoroughly convinced that the process of evolution would proceed until its consummation, that it would not destroy itself. As a consequence, he never really entertained the challenge of species destruction as Ferkiss and others lay it upon us. The history of man in the twentieth century, if Teilhard is correct in his interpretation, discloses to us the greatest challenge to survival that the human species has ever faced—the challenge to develop a species-system awareness which will enable the species to move toward unity, protect individual integrity, and maintain proper interrelationships with the environment. Teilhard devoted his energies, by and large, to painting murals depicting the future that would be realized if the challenge were met, as well as to drawing useful maps describing the routes toward that future. Together, murals and maps make sense of the human journey from prehistory to posthistory. If it is true that he failed to sense accurately the strength of the species' death wish that could stymie the entire human enterprise—if this be true, it does not annul Teilhard's vision, or his effort, but it does raise a number of searching questions that lead us directly to the philosophical, spiritual, and ethical questions of the next chapters.

III

"An Irreversibly Personalizing Universe"

Perhaps we can best summarize Teilhard's system of thought at the present stage of our analysis by quoting from the last pages of his masterwork:

> To make room for thought in the world, I have needed to "interiorize" matter: to imagine an energetics of the mind; to conceive a noogenesis rising upstream against the flow of entropy; to provide evolution with a direction, a line of advance and critical points . . . (PM, 290).

The quotation includes all of the major steps in Teilhard's system that we have thus far considered. The rest of the sentence goes on to say that in order to make room for thought in the world, Teilhard also had "finally to make all things double back upon *someone*." We now turn our efforts to an understanding of what this final clause means. It is the capstone of his thought.

Thus far our discussion has spelled out, as the focus of Teilhard's entire endeavor, his efforts to make sense of his times—his categories of interpretation and the most immediate assumptions upon which those categories rest. In this connection, we have spoken of Teilhard's first major extrapolation, by which he begins with the relatively brief history of consciousness in the evolutionary development of life, climaxing in man, and then projects forward and backward according to his law of complexity/consciousness, interpreting the events of the first half of the twentieth century as a critical phase of humankind's socialization, the complexification of the entire species to the point of species self-awareness. As accurate as it may be, however, to say that this effort "to discover a general significance in events" is the focus of all Teilhard's efforts, there is much more to his life and work. There is more, precisely because he was a full and integrated human being, who demanded that an interpretation of the times had to discover a significance that is genuinely whole. This meant for him a significance that covered all of the most fundamental questions of human existence that are brought together in the present age, including the questions of where the evolutionary process of complexification came from and where it is finally tending. Anyone who has attempted to explain history in such full terms has been caught up in the same quest for ultimate categories that can move through and beyond "the economic causes of ... " and "the social-political causes of ...." Toynbee, Spengler, Dewey, Hegel, Henry Adams, Karl Marx—these and others have found themselves faced with the same challenge.

We have noted at several points already that Teilhard could not escape the metaphysical dimension, even when he was dealing with what might be considered the most naturalistic temporal and spatial realities. In this, too, he found himself in a position not unusual among interpreters of human events. When he moved to the consideration of the larger issues that was necessary for a genuinely full interpretation of those events, however, he engaged in reflection that is plainly and unmistakably metaphysical (if—recalling our comments and Barbour's insights, discussed in Chapter I—we can define metaphysics in the tradition that ties it to empirical fact and inductive reasoning). We will not give much attention to the question of whether Teilhard's metaphysics determined his interpretation of contemporary events or whether that metaphysics grew out of the prior interpretation. It is certainly plausible, in light of his personal biography, to judge that he brought certain predilections with him to his interpretation of events, and this may become even clearer in the present chapter. For our purposes, we may assume that concrete interpretation of event and metaphysical assumption went hand in hand. And as a third companion to both interpretation and metaphysics stands Teilhard's religious faith and mystical sensitivity, as Chapter IV will suggest. I have chosen to emphasize the interpretation of current history as the focus of Teilhard's enterprise, but the other dimensions of the man are inseparably part of the total network of ideas and life that made the focus what it was. Other interpreters have chosen to center on the metaphysics or the religious faith and mysticism. That the three factors belong inextricably together is beyond dispute.

A. The Second Extrapolation: Personal Universe

We used the term "first major extrapolation" to refer to Teilhard's projection of the process of complexification, backward and forward from that segment of the evolutionary process that engendered consciousness and brought it to culmination in man. That extrapolation raises certain issues which make it clear that that first extrapolation cannot stand alone as a self-sustaining assertion about the nature of reality, organic or inorganic, human or prehuman. The process of complexification, as Teilhard sets it forth, asserts unequivocally that life, particularly human life, is caught up in a thrust toward centration—that is, a thrust toward ever more intense focusing upon the substance of identity that makes for personality. To be a centered entity or person is to possess clarity of meaning and identity. The enemies of centeredness are diffuseness, ambiguousness, mere conglomeration—in human beings, the feeling that things are coming apart at the seams. As human life grows in its centeredness, clarity, and identity, it grows in the lucidity of meaning that makes for fuller authenticity as a person. To speak of *personalizing* is to refer to this drive toward more intense self-consciousness and centeredness that makes for personal identity. Teilhard's category of complexification underscored the collective context of this personalizing thrust—individuals grow in authentic personality in solidarity with other individuals, and the species *as a species* grows more centered and thus personalized. This is what *convergence* in the species refers to.

The use of the terms "personalizing," "personalization," and "personal" are open to confusion and a variety of interpretations. Teilhard himself is not unambiguous in his use of them. In this chapter and the next, however, we interpret them to refer to *the process in which the elements of personhood grow more intense and approach their consummation*. These elements are the ones we have referred to here: consciousness, self-consciousness, and centeredness or focused meaning. It is important to note two points: (1) Teilhard is referring to a *process*, by which the personal grows and is perfected, rather than to a static concept of a person who possesses fixed characteristics. (2) He is not speaking only about the formation of individual human persons. The personalizing process operates both at the prehuman and the posthuman level. At the prehuman level, the process brings about the intensification of centeredness and consciousness that serves as springboard for the emergence of human personhood. At the posthuman level, Teilhard is not projecting the image of a human person forward when he speaks of the noosphere and its development; he is not picturing the universe in terms of anthropomorphisms. On the contrary, the personalizing process that has resulted in the formation of individual human persons at the human level goes on to a more intense stage of development that acts upon the entire species and will bring about a new phenomenon. This new phenomenon is personal and personalizing, because it embodies the elements of personhood carried to a higher power, but it is not a simple projection upon the cosmos of the image of a human person. This, at least, is our interpretation of Teilhard's somewhat ambiguous discussions.

This emphasis upon personalization, when it is made central in the way that Teilhard makes it, raises the question of whether all of reality is personalizing, both the inorganic and organic material world prior to man, within which he was evolved, and also the ultimate reality of the world and its future, in the context of which man will live out his future and meet his end. Teilhard's theory of complexification, with its assumptions concerning the law of complexity/consciousness, the "within" of things, and radial energy, amounts to a strong assertion that the world of organic and inorganic matter, the prehuman level, has always been oriented around the thrust toward personalization—even if that thrust remained nothing more than an unrealized potentiality at the lower levels on the evolutionary scale. Teilhard's extrapolation included, thus, a reading backward down the evolutionary past of the world, to trace the potentiality and the *telos* which served as the basis for personalization at the human level.

But what about the fundamental character of the world and its future? This is the ultimate milieu within which man lives out his career, the posthuman destiny toward which he is moving. Teilhard projects a second major extrapolation to assert that the ultimate character of the world is also personalizing. In other words, the thrust toward personalization that stands at the very heart of man's nature finds a resonance, not only in the physical world out of which he has emerged but also in the very foundations of the cosmos and its future. Man lives in a personal universe, and Teilhard chose to underscore this conviction by projecting what may be his most famous and his most bewildering concept: the *point Omega*. He called this Omega the "hyper-personal," the personal carried to its ultimate of intensification, the personal to the "nth degree." Omega is the point at which the entire universe attains its consummation as ultimately centered, self-aware, and unified.

Teilhard was well aware that large segments of mankind do not conceive of the world and the process of life as personal in character.

He recognized that there were strong pressures upon man to conceive of ultimate reality as depersonalized or impersonal in character. He considered this to be one of the causes for the demoralization of mankind, as well as one of the chief reasons why men could look to the collectivization of communism and fascism as the ultimate in human social and political organization. He ascribed the attractiveness of the depersonalized conception of the universe and man's destiny to the very factors that he argued against in the essays on planetization and in *Man's Place in Nature,* the preoccupation with quantity, the immense and the infinitesimal. The analytic method of science, "that marvelous instrument of scientific research to which we owe all our advances," has broken things down into their smallest units, allowing thus "one soul after another to escape, leaving us confronted with a pile of dismantled machinery and evanescent particles" (PM, 257 f.). We are so impressed with analysis that we have enthroned it as king, and at the same time destroyed personality. In addition, our discovery of the universe around us, with increasing knowledge of the planets and the galaxies, has brought a chilling sense of our own smallness in contrast with the dimensions of the cosmos.

What seems to be the only reality that survives the analysis of the infinitesimal and the immense? "Energy—that floating, universal entity from which all emerges and into which all falls back as into an ocean; energy, the new spirit; energy, the new god. So, at the world's Omega, as at its Alpha, lies the Impersonal" (PM, 258). Energy, blind force—these give shape to our conception of ultimate reality, with the consequence that personality seems to be an epiphenomenon, doomed to pass away. "We have lost both respect for the person and understanding of his true nature" (PM, 258). The impersonal lacks the intense centeredness that provides the meaning or identity that stands at the heart of personalization.

Teilhard considered this to be intolerable, because it laid down a fundamental incongruity between the human being and the rest of reality, a dissonance rather than a resonance. We end up, he writes, by saying to ourselves that when we center on ourselves, when we say "I," we are engaging in the egocentric activity by which the self

> closes the door on all the rest and succeeds in setting himself up at the antipodes of the All. In the opposite direction we conceive the "ego" to be diminishing and eliminating itself, with the trend to what is most real and most lasting in the world, namely, the Collective and the Universal. Personality is seen as a specifically cor-

puscular and ephemeral property; a prison from which we must try to escape (PM, 258).

Teilhard is challenging those who build a model or hypothesis of impersonality—such as the concept of energy or force—and use it as the key for understanding the world and its movement toward its future; among these he includes particularly the Marxists. The chief objection he raises to such a model, besides what he considers its demoralizing consequences upon mankind, is that it is impossible to "think" of the universe under this category, since it demands that we finally either ignore or degrade our own humanity and its place within the scheme of things (built as that humanity is upon consciousness and personality). "It would manifestly be an error," he says, "to extend the curve of hominization in the direction of a state of diffusion. It is only in the direction of hyper-reflection—that is to say, hyper-personalization—that thought can extrapolate itself" (PM, 258 f.). Human thought simply cannot look at *ultimate* reality through the end of the telescope that depicts the immense, the infinitesimal, and the impersonal, because to do so is literally antihuman.

In an important essay written in 1936 (and unfortunately still untranslated), *Esquisse d'un univers personnel* ("Sketch of a Personal Universe"), Teilhard made his own proposal very clear—namely, that he intended "to construct a figure [could we say a 'model'?] of the physical world that is oriented upon the human person, chosen as the element which is significant for the whole system" (Oe VI, 70). This is in effect exactly what Teilhard did to carry out his first major extrapolation, and he interpreted the more proximate realities of evolutionary development and contemporary history in terms of this model. Now he carries out the same operation, raising the extrapolation to a higher power, in order to interpret the entire movement of the world and its future. When we do this, he says, we see that the "I" and the "All" are not opposed to each other, but rather, "the noosphere (and more generally the world) represent a whole that is not only closed but also *centered*" (PM, 259). As such it engenders consciousness and personality. The conclusion is that space and time "must somewhere ahead become involuted to a point which we might call *Omega*, which fuses and consumes them integrally in itself" (*ibid.*).

It *is* possible to "think" or conceive of the universe on the basis of the model of personalization without denying any of the scientific knowledge we have gained through the end of the telescope that reveals its immense and infinitesimal dimensions.

In the perspective of a noogenesis, time and space become truly humanized—or rather super-humanized. Far from being mutually exclusive, the Universal and Personal (that is to say, the "centered") grow in the same direction and culminate simultaneously in each other. It is therefore a mistake to look for the extension of our being or of the noosphere in the Impersonal. The Future-Universal could not be anything else but the Hyper-Personal—at the Omega Point (PM, 260).

In his discussion of contemporary events, he asserted that Man's political and social existence as a species had to become both collectivized and personalized, unification with the preservation of that incommunicable uniqueness that gives each man his identity as a person. Now he has projected this image of unification-within-personhood onto the cosmic screen and formulated the final destiny of the world in its terms. This is how Teilhard avoids what he calls a distorted pantheism and mysticism. Man is not absorbed into a final All, as a drop of ink is dispersed in the ocean. Our centeredness is our very self and personality, and the Omega respects this. Omega is consciousness, but it preserves all consciousnesses. It is centered, but as a *"distinct Center at the core of a system of centers;* a grouping in which personalization of the All and personalizations of the elements reach their maximum, simultaneously and without merging"* (PM, 258 f.). Omega refers not only to the world's final destiny, but is also an image of the ultimate meaning of the *present* world process (PM, 268 f.).

The Teilhardian Omega concept has baffled many of his students. It is a profound and mysterious concept, and we certainly have not exhausted its depths here in any respect. But we can understand it more easily if we do not conceive of it literally, if we do not attempt to locate and objectify the Omega point. Above all, we must not make it into a "highest person" in the form of a human person writ large. Rather, we must conceive of it as the "figure" or model—consistent with Teilhard's entire system—that Teilhard needed as a basis for "thinking" the universe and its destiny. It is not for that reason less real. It was very real for Teilhard, this personal reality in which everything moves and has its being; it was at the heart of his religious experience and mystical vision. But it could be thought or conceived by the human mind only by projecting a model or image which could suggest its outlines and thus make sense. That is what Teilhard had in mind in the last clause of the summarizing quotation with which we opened this chapter: "I have needed . . . finally to make all things double back upon *someone"*—the personal. And this is the key to understanding the final sentence in *The Phenomenon of Man*, which stands as the motto for this chapter: "The only universe capable of containing the human person is an irreversibly 'personalizing' universe" (PM, 290). That is to say, the only universe that the human mind can conceive or "think" without having to abandon the centrality of his own uniqueness as a person is a universe that is itself ultimately personalizing. When Omega is viewed in these terms, we can understand how it can be both final end and present depth of the world process, in the same way, as we shall see, as Christ is both end and depth (see Chapter IV).

Teilhard's interpretation of contemporary events has led us to this—a challenge to project a final image for conceiving the nature of the world and its ultimate future. This challenge was implicit all along, but the formulation of the point Omega makes it explicit. If we are to speak of the "promise" of Teilhard, the bluntness of this challenge is certainly a part of that promise. Teilhard is not alone in saying that the personal is the most adequate model of thought upon which to build our understanding of reality. The process philosophers, including Alfred North Whitehead and Charles Hartshorne, the theologians who follow in their train, John Cobb and Schubert Ogden (to mention only two), other theologians such as John A. T. Robinson, Leslie Dewart, and Michael Novak, and, indeed, the classical trinitarian theology of the Christian tradition—all of these are important sources of thought that concur in suggesting that the model of the personal (to be sure, they do not all mean exactly the same thing by "personal") is significant for understanding ultimate reality.[1] But there are also important counter proposals that vie for our attention, and we must survey, at least, the state of the argument between these two camps. Before we can do that, however, it will be helpful to consider two additonal motifs that belong to the basic assertion of a personalizing universe, even as they figure in the modes of thought that oppose Teilhard's position.

B. Is Life Trustworthy?

At the very heart of Teilhard's perception that the Omega (or something like it) is a necessary concept if man is to be able to think aright about his destiny and the world's is the concern for the resonance or dissonance between the human enterprise and "the way things are out there"—that is, between man and his world, between man's career and the future of the world. If there is an essential dissonance between man and the world, between man and whatever future awaits him and the world, then the process of life in which man participates is ultimately untrustworthy and unreliable, and the absurdity that presents itself to man is, quite literally for Teilhard, *unthinkable*. Teilhard was himself certain that human existence would prove impossible for man to continue if he could not discern the reliability of the evolutionary process; and by reliability, we mean the existence of a resonance or a meaningful correlation between man's being and the world itself. He puts it thus:

> In broad terms it may be affirmed that the Human, having become aware of its uncompleted state, cannot lend itself without reluctance, still less give itself with passion, to any course that may attract it unless there be some kind of discernible and definitive consummation to be looked for at the end, if only as a limit. Above all it rejects dispersal and dissolution and the circle from which there is no escape (FM, 277).

More systematically, Teilhard speaks of a "principle of the conservation of the personal" which is essential to the continuation of evolutionary process beyond the present state (Oe, VI, 198 ff.; FM, 206 f.). This principle has three forms: (1) the movement toward heightened consciousness and complexification is irreversible—that is, it cannot be turned back, but rather all of its gains are preserved and enhanced in further forward movement; (2) the impersonal state of some realities will be finally transformed into personal reality; (3) the nucleus of every individual personality is immortal, and it will retain its uniqueness even in the transformation into the hyperpersonalized state. Recalling the distinction between the "without" and the "within" of things, Teilhard sets this principle of the conservation of the personal, pertinent as it is for the universe of the spirit, in parallelism with the principle of the conservation of energy which pertains to the physical dimension.

This unshakable belief in the reliability of the life process is important for Teilhard's system of thought, since he employs it as a criterion by which he judges the value of the events and forces he sees in the world about him, and by which he discerns what movements are in the vanguard of the evolution of the noosphere and which are reactionary or obstructive. An essay that dates from 1939, "The Grand Option," is instructive in this regard. In it Teilhard spells out the options that man has in assessing the critical phase of socialization that mankind is now passing through. The first alternative is pessimism or optimism, focusing in the question, "Is it better to Be than not to Be?" Teilhard considers this question—despite its abstract, metaphysical form—to be a concrete question that every man must face and answer for himself. He believes that the world is divided into two camps on this question, "those who deny that there is any significance or value in the state of Being, and therefore no Progress" (among these he includes the figure of Sisyphus, who slaves day after day in pointless labor), and those who "believe in the possibility and the rewards of a higher state of consciousness" (FM, 42). The first group of men must desert life, he says, since they are lodged in incoherence and disintegration." Teilhard follows the second group.

The second alternative is between the optimism on the one hand that is confident of the progress of life, but only by escaping the bonds of matter (by asceticism or mysticism) and withdrawing from this world to await the consummation, and the optimism on the other that sees ultimate value "in the tangible evolution of things." The latter position is Teilhard's, and he follows it to the third alternative, between those who are pluralists and thus seek consummation in individualism, shunning socialization, and those who pursue unity and thus support socialization, because they seek consummation in the convergence of mankind.

These alternative assessments, in turn, present four possibilities to man for responding to the phenomenon of socialization: suicide, withdrawal, efforts to fulfill oneself through egoistic individualism and segregation, or plunging "resolutely into the stream of the whole in order to become part of it." One's response must be intentional; it is not enough to say that one's choice is merely a matter of temperament.

> For let us face it: to each of the four choices we have outlined there must necessarily correspond a Universe of an especial kind— disorderly or ordered, exhausted or still young, divergent or convergent. And of these four kinds of Universe, *only one can exist at a time—only one is true* (FM, 48).

It is here that Teilhard brings up the question of a criterion for making the decision. We are like "the captain of a ship heading for a prescribed harbor"; what will guide us? Teilhard lays down, very significantly, his choice of criterion—it must be either entropy or life: either the processes of the universe are running backward toward diffusion and disin-

[73]

tegration or they are moving forward toward increasing centeredness and personality—that is, *toward life*. In an argument reminiscent of his comments in *The Phenomenon of Man*, where he insisted that man could not even conceive of the universe on the model of impersonality, Teilhard suggests that the category of life is simply more useful than the category of entropy for conceiving the nature of the universe. "For the purposes of human action, entropy . . . is without meaning" (FM, 49). (We can imagine, for example, that both the middle class that is attempting to maintain present society and the radical revolutionaries who are trying to alter it would agree with this maxim.)

Teilhard then proceeds to reduce all of the alternatives he has suggested, and he does so on the basis of what we might call the "argument from life"—namely, that the alternatives must be synthesized or eliminated according to how adequately they serve the purposes of maintaining and increasing the complexification of life. Suicide is thus eliminated. In one of his mystical allusions, he argues that withdrawal is not tenable unless it is a withdrawal to a new phase of being that the material world will eventually evolve into; immediate or premature withdrawal is out of the question. Individualistic separation must be rejected, because it does not serve the purposes of life conceived under the rubric of complexification, even though its concern for the preservation of the individual center of selfhood is valid. Individualism points essentially to separation and divergence in the universe, and divergence is biologically a final principle of disintegration and death. In the service of life, Teilhard discerns the superiority of the responses of love and the movement toward unity without totalitarianism.

At one level, Teilhard's argument here is a circular one. He has argued that if the evolution of life and the movement of contemporary history are what he says they are, then the concepts of point Omega and the reliability of the life process are the only viable ones, when compared to the alternatives. Then, however, he utilizes those concepts to substantiate the very interpretation of contemporary history that engendered them. He has, in other words, begged the very question that he seeks to answer. However, Teilhard is operating here at a level where his argument is not invalidated simply because it has a certain circularity. Teilhard's argument here stands or falls according to whether its substance is fundamentally challenging to us or not. Its challenge lies in two questions which Teilhard poses sharply. The first question is whether it is or is not possible for man to conceive a unified view of the universe on the premise that the universe proceeds counter to personalization, the basic thrust of human existence. (For example, Is the universe essentially impersonal? Is either entropy or energy descriptive of the final state of reality?) The second question is whether it is safe to assume that man lives in a world that is in fundamental congruity with him and his existence. Is man living "at home" in this world, or is the world and its future basically hostile to him? This question deals with the reliability of human perception and knowledge and the way in which man's mind functions. The promise of Teilhard at this point may lie not so much in his being right or wrong, but in the fact that he brings us up so sharply, so sensitively, and so intelligently before these unavoidable questions. But before we can pursue this matter further, we must probe one remaining facet of Teilhard's system of thought.

C. The Last Word: Good or Evil?

One of the most frequently discussed aspects of Teilhard's thought is his treatment of what is called his belief in progress, or his "optimism," and the ensuing concepts of good and evil that follow from it. We have reported that his first major confrontation with ecclesiastical censorship came on the issue of original sin and evil. There have been a long list of theological critics since that time who have criticized Teilhard's views on evil. It is often said, as Dobzhansky does, that "Optimism is a commodity in short supply in the modern world. Teilhard's optimism is surely one of the reasons for the wide appeal of his thought."[2] If we are to summarize the arguments and still do justice to Teilhard, several things must be said.

First of all, Teilhard's alleged optimism is intimately bound up with his concept of progress. Teilhard is not umambiguously clear on this question, and there is no doubt that he was personally convinced that the evolutionary tendencies he had sketched concerning the formation of the noosphere, man's convergence and ultrapersonalization, would in fact someday actualize themselves. On the other hand, it is also just as clear that he had no blind, naïve confidence in what we ordinarily call "progress." He discussed progress in three essays that are gathered in *The Future of Man*, and he develops a carefully defined concept of it. Progress does not mean that evil will disappear from the world. He does not use the term in the traditional eighteenth- and nineteenth-century liberal sense of moral improvement. Progress refers to the increase of consciousness, particularly self-consciousness as it moves from individual self-awareness to species self-awareness.[3] Progress is movement along the line of complexification, and that movement is slow, just as all organic processes are slow (FM, 19, 69).

Secondly, Teilhard's confidence in the processes of life did not grow out of any personal lack of acquaintance with evil or a personally superficial understanding of evil. Although his formal writings might not disclose his own serious personal grappling with evil, frustration, injustice, inner anxiety and turmoil, and loss, his letters do. Several interpreters of Teilhard, notably Robert Speaight, Christopher Mooney, and Henri de Lubac, have filled out our picture on this score. Teilhard was himself subject to depression; he saw most of his closest family die during his lifetime; he knew the brutality of war firsthand; and, of course, he knew what it meant to suffer alienation and exile from family, church, and nation. He knew the bitterness of having his most important life work—his major writings—stifled and hidden from the world by unjust censorship. He faces squarely the question of whether mankind will not destroy itself rather than fulfill its evolutionary destiny.

Thirdly, it is true that Teilhard possessed a certain stoic resilience and manly zest for enduring hardship that sometimes appear to take evil less seriously than they ought. Those who look for a bleeding heart as a sign of humanness will not (and have not) found what they are looking for in Teilhard. He himself laments on occasion that he did not enter into his fellows' suffering as he ought. On the other hand, Teilhard had a very clear vision of the evil intrinsic to the process of complexification. He did not have to find ways to insert evil into an otherwise painless process of development. This evil was intrinsic as weakness, distortion, destruction, misuse and abuse, and obstruction of growth. These terms have put off the traditional theologians, because they seem pale; they are also reminiscent in tone of a diluted liberalism that many detest. We might suggest, however, that when we consider that the process of complexification is the life process, the terms mentioned above take on all the trauma and terror that we associate with psychological illness and social malfunctioning. When we consider just what "obstruction" and "destruction" mean, for example, in the process of a child growing from adolescence into adulthood, or of a man coming to terms with achievement and failure, or of a man and a woman forging a marriage, we know that those terms are not pale in their significance. When we consider what misuse and abuse mean in the course of men's personal relations with one another, or in man's relationship with his environment, we understand how deeply those terms can cut. One sometimes has the impression that Teilhard's critics are aiming at the Olympian, patrician demeanor of his exterior when they accuse him of overlooking evil. It may be that his descriptions make evil seem so *intrinsic* in the life process that we are tempted to consider them superficial. Yet we find, upon closer inspection, that his perspective throws light on our common experience. We acknowledge, for example, the severe pain and trauma that afflict the adolescent's entrance into maturity, and yet we also express optimism that the adolescent *will* survive the passage. This may explain why Teilhard could say, in the appendix that he added in 1948 to *The Phenomenon of Man*, that even as he affirmed confidence in the processes of life, "it still remains true that, even in the view of the mere biologist, the human epic resembles nothing so much as a way of the Cross" (PM, 313). Few of his critics have dealt meaningfully with that statement.

Fourthly, we must give at least cursory attention to the elaborate theory of original sin and evil which went along with Teilhard's personal attitudes towards evil. It is the theory that first brought Teilhard into difficulty with his superiors and one that has received scrutiny from friends and foes alike who have entered into Teilhard's controversy. The basic document in the controversy is *Réflexions sur le Péché originel*, written in 1947 but never edited for publication during his lifetime and still not in print, just as the 1924 essay that originally brought the ill favor of the Church has never seen the light of publication. Fortunately, Georges Crespy has summarized the more recent essay in English.[4]

Invoking some support in the traditions of Eastern theology, in contrast to Western Augustinianism, Teilhard insists that the Fall must not be viewed as a localized historical event in the lives of the first human pair, but rather as "a general condition affecting the totality of history" and therefore a prehistorical occasion. By placing the fall into the realm of prehistory, Teilhard brings evil into conjunction with his distinctive theory of creation. (Elements of this theory of creation are contained in Chapter IV of *Science and Christ*.) Creation is a process of *uniting*, and he speaks of it, therefore, in terms of union rather than in terms of being.[5] In a complex argument, Teilhard speaks of God "opposing himself" in such a manner as to call into existence a disordered void which he arranges and unifies. All of the created order emerges from this "creatable void," as it moves toward ever increasing unification.

Evil and sinfulness emerge as soon as the process of unification begins, because that process is, as Crespy paraphrases,

> impregnated with pains and errors. It is statistically inevitable that in the course of the journey some local disorders will appear, and consequently there will result *collective disordered conditions* with pain in the midst of the living and sin in the midst of man.[6]

Evil is thus the inevitable by-product of creation itself, but at the same time is thoroughly subordinate to the creative activity of God and to the destiny toward which he is moving his creation.

Teilhard's theory of original sin and evil runs into immediate problems. It implicates God as the author of evil, since the appearance of evil is coincident with the beginning of His creative activity. Critics of Teilhard have rejected the impersonalizing effect of his theory, on the grounds that it does not do justice to the personal identification that every individual feels with sin and to the personal guilt that ensues.[7] On the other hand, the theory does perform several intellectual functions rather well. It frees us from the notion that the physical world is in itself evil, since evil is part of the process of the development of matter, but not an attribute of matter. Teilhard's theory also forestalls any easy optimism that would posit a world free from evil; it is important to understand this feature of his thinking, because it indicates how far his ideas of progress are from liberal conceptions of moral improvement. By placing evil within the creative process, Teilhard underscores its intrinsic presence throughout the created world. Finally, Teilhard succeeds in recapturing the genuine meaning of the biblical myth of the Fall, by freeing evil from an original couple named Adam and Eve. He reminds us that the biblical myth is speaking about a universal human condition of sinfulness and not about a historically datable event in the past.

Professor Crespy has epitomized Teilhard's understanding of evil in a manner that relates this aspect of his thought to his total vision:

> Teilhard is right once again when he affirms that evil is such only evolutively, that is, only relatively to future good. Evil is evil only as a consequence of a passion for the best. In other words, once again there is evil only if the world is going somewhere, if it has meaning and direction. And then evil is the *nondirection of this direction and the nonmeaning of this meaning.*[8]

Fifthly, Teilhard's insistence that evolutionary processes will ultimately reach consummation must be held in its proper unity with his exhortations for men to renew their will and engage in energetic action. At times, he does seem to make the movement of evolution an autonomous force, above and beyond human efforts. He did not, however, look with indifference upon the power and significance of human decision and activity. On the contrary, he put a high premium on human efforts in support of the process of evolution, because he knew that man *could* decide against the processes of his own development and that he could (and indeed *did* many times) obstruct that development.

For Teilhard, however, it was one thing to look realistically at the forces of evil and disintegration, to root them in the very processes of complexification (he does both), and quite another to decide that evil would prevail. It was still another thing to plan the actions of one's life in a manner consistent with the conclusion that evil is pre-eminent. Teilhard refused to acknowledge that the processes of complexification could fail. When he considered opposing modes of thought and life, such as the Existentialism of Jean-Paul Sartre, he could see the problem clearly:

> In speaking of the rise of terrestrial psychic temperature I have always assumed that in the Noosphere, as in the Biosphere, the need and the will to grow both remain constant. There can be no natural selection, still less reflective invention, if the individual is not inwardly intent upon "super-living," or at least upon survival. No evolutionary mechanism can have any power over a cosmic matter if it is entirely passive, less still if it is opposed to it. But the possibility has to be faced of Mankind falling suddenly out of love with its own destiny. This disenchantment would be conceivable, and indeed inevitable, if as a result of growing reflection we came to believe that our end could only be collective death in an hermetically sealed world. Clearly in face of so appalling a discovery the psychic mechanism of evolution would come to a stop, undermined and shattered in its very substance, despite all the violent tuggings of the chain of planetary in-folding (FM, 296).

This eloquent passage dates from 1950. But Teilhard cannot accept the eventualities about which he writes so movingly here. In light of his approach to the personalizing character of reality and the reliability of the life process, we are not surprised to find Teilhard saying (in the paragraph following the one I have just cited) that when he reflects on the destruction of the evolutionary process, the question that arises is how life "might be extinguished on earth without being continued elsewhere. *Having once become reflective it cannot acquiesce in its total disappearance without biologically contradicting itself"* (FM, 296, italics added).

The argument recurs; the premises are the same. The relation between man and his world, throughout the evolutionary process, is one of congruence and resonance. It follows, as night follows day, that man cannot then conceive of the universe except in conjunction with its essentially personalizing character, the trustworthiness of its processes, specifically the process of life, and the final consummation of those processes, which means that good and not evil is finally predominant. Teilhard brings us up short, once again, before the decision as to whether evil or good is the last word. It is not the question of whether evil is real and deadly, of whether one ought to take it seriously, but rather of whether it is the final word for man and the universe. This question turns out, of course, to be synonymous with the previous two, since the consummation of the evolutionary process, over any forces of evil and obstructions, means the realization of the hyperpersonal, Omega, and this in turn entails the trustworthiness of the process of life.

D. The Nature of the Controversy

The promise of Teilhard in respect to his affirmation that "the only universe capable of containing the human person is an irreversibly personalizing universe" lies chiefly in his success in putting the questions and stating the issues so clearly that the fundamental challenge of his thought is unmistakable—even for those who disagree with his position and finally reject him.

One of the most important recent statements of the position that opposes Teilhard's is that of Albert Camus. It is instructive that Sisyphus is the figure whom Teilhard chooses as the epitome of the hopeless, antlike slave, who can see no hope in the movement of evolution and human history. Sisyphus is also Camus' prototypical figure. For Tielhard, Sisyphus' position is untenable; for Camus, it is not a question of Sisyphus' position being impossible—rather, his fate, rolling the stone up the mountain perpetually, only to have it roll down again each time, is the way things are, there is no other way. Camus and Teilhard were concerned with the same question. Camus writes: "There is but one truly serious philosophical problem, and that is suicide.

Judging whether life is or is not worth living amounts to answering the fundamental question of philosophy."[9] Camus formulates a category of the Absurd, as the fundamental category for interpreting the world and its movement. Absurdity is the occasion for considering suicide. Two eloquent quotations put his views clearly:

> I said that the world is absurd, but I was too hasty. This world in itself is not reasonable, that is all that can be said. But what is absurd is the confrontation of this irrational and the wild longing for clarity whose call echoes in the human heart. The absurd depends as much on man as on the world. For the moment it is all that links them together.[10]

> ... man stands face to face with the irrational. He feels within him his longing for happiness and for reason. The absurd is born of this confrontation between the human need and the unreasonable silence of the world. This must not be forgotten. This must be clung to because the whole consequence of a life can depend on it. The irrational, the human nostalgia, and the absurd that is born of their encounter—these are the three characters in the drama that must necessarily end with all the logic of which an existence is capable.[11]

Camus nevertheless decided *against* suicide and *for* a courageous ethical life in behalf of one's fellow man. The *logic* of existence demanded this. The chief character in his novel, *The Plague*, epitomizes his position. Dr. Rieux would not believe in God, because the concept of God was used to cover up the reality of the absurd situation. He muses that "since the order of the world is shaped by death, mightn't it be better for God if we refuse to believe in Him and struggle with all our might against death, without raising our eyes toward the heaven where He sits in silence."[12] But this struggle looks for no victories: "Rieux believed himself to be on the right road—in fighting against creation as he found it."[13]; "no peace was possible to him henceforth, any more than there can be an armistice for a mother bereaved of her son or for a man who buries his friend."[14]

The two positions are clear—both held by Frenchman near the end of the first half of our century: The one holds that man stands in congruity with evolution and world history, a congruity based on the personalizing character of the world, resonating to his own essential personhood; he is enabled therefore to give himself to the processes of evolution, confident of consummation; the other holds to an intrinsic incongruity between man and reality "out there," since the world is silent to man's cries for meaning, and even though man must give himself to the struggle for human existence—in the face of all odds—he is fighting against creation, and he has no hope of victory or even intelligibility in his struggle; the struggle is an end in itself. The real nub of Teilhard's disagreement with Camus is at the point where Camus insists upon the absurdity of the world—"this confrontation between the human need and the unreasonable silence of the world." Indeed, Teilhard would most likely ask whether Camus has a world, or even a concept of a world.

In raising this question, Teilhard is applying pressure at two points. First, he is insisting that the ability to provide a view of the world that is *coherent with* or *congruous with* man's own understanding of the essence of his selfhood and his position within the world is a major criterion for evaluating the religions, philosophies, and world views that call for our attention and commitment. Here, as we have noted elsewhere, Teilhard combines the empirical with the speculative. The understanding of one's own essential selfhood is rooted in concrete experience, whereas the view of the world that must be coherent with that experience is quite speculative. Teilhard's *method* is of interest at this point. He is focusing upon the question of how man's mind works, particularly in its efforts to "think" about the world, the future of the cosmos, the universe, and ultimates of any kind. Teilhard is presupposing, as did many classical philosophers and theologians and not a few contemporary thinkers, as well, that man thinks by analogy about these realities, that he constructs models and uses them as interpretive principles for gaining insight into the structure of the world. Here we gain a glimpse into the relationship between Teilhard's vision and scientific fact. The decision to use certain specific analogies or models for understanding the larger realities of world, God, and future cannot be validated by logic or experiment. Teilhard's model of the personal, as we have defined it here, consisting of consciousness, self-consciousness, centeredness, and the meaning that gives identity, is validated or invalidated by the same canons of persuasiveness as any other. It stands or falls on its ability to make cogent sense out of the concrete facts of experience that every man knows or can observe. Teilhard insists that an analogy or model other than the personal one violates the basic structure of man's mind, because it leads inevitably to a world view that turns on an axis other than that which comprises man's own selfhood. This view implies a confidence in man's reflective capacity and in the congruity between man and his world which many will not be able to affirm—and they will take Camus' side.

Second, Teilhard is implying that this question of the reliability of the process of life is the crucial question for man. This question of reliability is really the other side of the issue concerning the congruity between man and his world. If the process of life is reliable, man's mind will not be out of kilter in its perceptions of the world and its future. Analogical projections *will* be credible and reliable. Teilhard is really transforming the "God-question," whether God exists and what his will for man is, away from its focus on the existence of God *as such* to the focus on the trustworthiness of the world and its processes of life. The bare bones of this "God-argument" are this: If the process of evolution is ultimately trustworthy, then the question arises as to the cause and order of that trustworthiness, to which the concept of God is a reasonable, if not the *most reasonable*, answer.

This transformation of the site where the God-questioning should take place is much more relevant to contemporary men than older traditional arguments for or against God. Professor George Wald, Nobel Laureate biologist at Harvard, has eloquently expressed the contemporary concern. Our generation, he writes, is "a generation that isn't sure it has a future."[15] That is to say, our generation is not certain that the process of life is trustworthy even to sustain us, let alone enhance our personalization. A number of younger theologians have also transformed the God-questioning in a way that parallels Teilhard, with variations of their own. Schubert Ogden, in his discussion of Sartre, for example, makes a criticism that mirrors Teilhard's. He asks whether Sartre does not, by his tenacious insistence on moral responsibility, articulate a witness to the congruity between man and his world and hence a witness to its reliability and thereby a "strange witness of unbelief" to God's existence.[16] Michael Novak has argued in a similar fashion concerning the grounds for belief in his book, *Belief and Unbelief*, as has J. A. T. Robinson in his *Exploration into God*.

In his formal writings, Teilhard reveals that he is cognizant of the position represented by Camus and others, like Sartre, but he does not reveal deep empathy with it or insight into it. The major weakness in his approach, which seems to be intrinsic to his style of argument, is that he seems unable to appreciate the courage and sense of duty in Camus' position. He does not seem to have considered that a Camus could be just as committed to the human enterprise as he, *with contrary metaphysical assumptions* which deny the congruity between man and world. Teilhard's encounters with the Christian Existentialist Gabriel Marcel seem to indicate the same inability to get inside the opposing view, although Marcel seemed equally baffled by Teilhard.

The considerations that arise from Teilhard's arguments with the Existentialists are also pertinent to his dialogue with the Marxists. The Marxists and the scientific humanists would take issue particularly with Teilhard's insistence upon the ultimately personalizing character of reality. They represent the position that uses the model of "process," "dialectic," "force," or "energy"—all impersonal—as the foundation upon which to build a view of the universe. Here again, however, the question of absurdity arises, since these positons must determine the status of the personal centeredness of human beings. If this centeredness is a "sport" or freak occurrence in nature, which does not find its final resonance in the nature of ultimate reality itself, then their philosophical conclusion approaches incongruity and absurdity. While it may not be as traumatic as that pictured by Camus, it is nevertheless just as disquieting unless one is willing to give up the demand for resonance between the personalizing process at work in man, on the one hand, and the world, on the other. Here, Teilhard's argument fares differently, because Marxists would not insist on the category of absurdity. As we will note in the next chapter, their humanistic concerns for the future of a world in which man is "at home," because he has overcome alienation, is quite apparent. Teilhard asks, nevertheless, whether their humanism can succeed when it is set within a world of basically impersonal process. Interestingly, Teilhard could admire the humanistic zeal of the Marxists, but he was blind to the same zeal among the Existentialists.

Whether we agree with Teilhard or not on these issues is not the most urgent question, ultimately, but rather the fact that he has pressed us so vigorously to face the issue. That so many of his younger contemporaries and members of the generation that succeeded his have taken up these same questions indicates how promising his line of questioning is. These men often bring more philosophical skill and historical knowledge to the task that he did. But few of them bring his breadth of mind, his scientific education, his religious nurture, or his broad experience to bear upon the questions.

IV

The Action That Super-Humanizes

How is it possible to come this far in our study without describing the depths and nuances of Teilhard's religious faith? How is it possible to picture the Jesuit father without immediately exploring his religious life? Clearly, it would be impossible to overlook for a moment Teilhard's faith, even though at first glance it might appear that we ourselves have painted a onesidedly intellectual picture of him. He was outspokenly Christian, unabashedly Jesuit. He could not tolerate a day passing without saying his Mass; when he was temporarily blinded on a field trip in China, his companion, Presbyterian George Barbour, was pressed into service to read his daily breviary to him. Henri de Monfried, with whom Teilhard sailed in his private boat on the Red Sea in 1928, has written a striking reminiscence of Teilhard's personal religious impact upon him:

> At night, lying on the deck of my boat, Teilhard and I would meditate on the infinity of the stars . . . . During this silent reverie, in which two men were able to understand and communicate with each other, I understood why Teilhard could look indulgently at his fellow men when they excite themselves to no purpose, and very often against all reason. How many unfortunate people, discouraged, embittered and revolted by the blind hostility of the mob, by injustice and want of understanding—how many of these disinherited men and women, perverted and brought near to destruction by a contempt for themselves, have been comforted and saved by this man with the clear regard who knew how to bring dead consciences to life, just as Jesus of Nazareth brought Lazarus back from the dead.[1]

There is no question that Teilhard's Christian faith was explicit and articulate in his very appearance and in his every thought and action. The question is, What sort of a Christian faith did he embody? When we examine the nature of his faith, it will be clearer why so little overt Christianity has appeared in our analysis thus far. Teilhard's Christian faith stands in the classical tradition known as Christian humanism. Christian humanism is often described in the Thomistic maxim, "Grace does not destroy nature, but perfects it." It is succinctly stated by Teilhard himself: "the guiding principles of Christ's religion are exactly the same as those in which we found the essence of human effort expressed . . . . Christianity is not only not opposed to Humanism but provides it with exactly the complement without which terrestrial faith cannot reach its full and complete development" (SC, 147). Teilhard took this position very seriously and apparently believed rather literally, as he wrote in 1933, that to "Christianize" the fundamental aims of the world and human existence is to "consummate" them, bring them to the same goal of fulfillment that they push toward inherently.

Such a position involves a two-way movement of thought. On the one hand, as Teilhard himself said, he doubtless would never have formulated his image of point Omega if his religious life and faith had not already convinced him of its reality (PM, 294). Christian humanism involves the tendency to read the human situation in light of the Christian vision which one brings to that situation. But, on the other hand, Teilhard plainly did not intend to do this in any simplistic sense. That is why he argued so vehemently at times that the Christian dare not overlook the intrinsic worth of the world and human effort and development, as if his Christian faith could somehow free him from having to give serious attention to that worth. In 1934, he wrote, "If, as a result of some interior revolution, I were successively to lose my faith in Christ, my faith in a personal God, my faith in the Spirit, I think I would still continue to believe in the World."[2] It is true that Teilhard believed that his Christian vision opened up for him a truer understanding of the world and of human existence, but nevertheless the God he knew was a God who participated fully in the material world and its development, and who was therefore *a God whom one could not know or relate to except as he knew and participated fully in the physical development of the world.* He wrote to a friend in 1949, "Let us fulfill humanity here on earth, so that Christ can come back."[3] For this reason, although Teilhard is obviously and totally a "Christian, a Catholic priest, and a Jesuit" (as Christopher Mooney puts it in his superb study of Teilhard's theological system), there is something that violates the logic of what he wanted to convey to his fellow men if we

[86]

approach him first in terms of his Christian faith and secondarily as a human being in search of understanding. The logic of his own personal biography began with the Sacred Heart of Jesus piety, but the testimony he labored to bring to his Church and to the world is not a replication of his own personal journey. The promise of Teilhard for the churches today and their theology, as well as his promise for all men, centers in the fact that he is perhaps the most forceful embodiment of Christian humanism since Friedrich Schleiermacher, who flourished in Berlin during the early 1800's—some might want to say since Leonardo da Vinci. The point is that Teilhard is the first truly monumental Christian humanist who was fully shaped by the modern scientific world view, fully at home in the piety and thought of Christianity, and who could discern what the outlines of the postmodern world would look like.

From this perspective, we must say that the "phenomenon of Teilhard" has been obscured by the fact that he broke upon the world's consciousness through the church, through ecclesiastical and theological friends who took up the cudgels against the ban of the censors. It is to be regretted that so much of the world's first impression of him was therefore filtered through the incredibly complicated French controversies concerning the orthodoxy of his religious faith. His American experience may perhaps have given him the opportunity to project his most authentic image—except, of course, that it deprived him of his French milieu—namely, as a humanist, a man of science and affairs, who expressed himself as a Christian. One wonders what would have happened if he had been permitted to come upon the scene more in the style of other recent humanists—as for example, a J. Robert Oppenheimer, a Loren Eiseley, a Dag Hammarskjöld, an Alfred North Whitehead, or an Arnold Toynbee—through the eloquent expression of his superb essays, supplementing and clarifying the complexities of his *Phenomenon of Man*, rather than through the apologetic editions prepared by his friends. This was the style in which his career began in France in the twenties. One can surmise that it was only the fame of his association with the team that discovered Peking Man that saved him from complete obscurity under the ban. (Considering, however, the conditions that he did have to face, we can express only gratitude and admiration to the group of friends that secured the editing and publication of so much of his work. Without them, Teilhard would still be unknown to us.)

Therefore, even though we cannot give proper space to the theology that complements his interpretation of history and his metaphysical assumptions, we are in a position to perceive accurately the context for his Christian theology and its function in his life and work. And since his religious faith both shares in and fulfills his knowledge of the physical world, there is a profound sense in which everything that we have discussed up to this point *is* Teilhard's theology.

Teilhard spoke of his Christian faith, in the Epilogue to *The Phenomenon of Man*, as a "confirmation" or "cross-check" for his phenomenological or "scientific" conclusions, particularly for the conception of the Omega point (PM, 298 f). In one of his later essays, he reflects on the fact that biology brings us to the conclusion that man is approaching a final unity through the totalizing and centrating movement of the evolutionary process, whereas in Christian doctrine we find the belief that "the human individual cannot perfect himself or fully exist except through the organic unification of all men in God" (FM, 223). He sees the two as complementary—"the critical point of maturation envisaged by science being simply the physical condition and experimental aspect of the critical point of the Parousia postulated and awaited in the name of Revelation" (FM, 223 f). These comments fit in well with what we know about Teilhard's obsession for unity. "To believe is to achieve an intellectual synthesis," he said at one point.[4] One of the most important functions of his understanding of Christ was to complete this intellectual synthesis. The fact that Christ embodied the unity and love of Omega gave Teilhard a means for completing the global synthetic science we spoke of in Chapter II. His understanding of Christ made it possible for him to move from scientific reason to Revelation as easily as he did.

A. Coherence in Human Action

The complexity of Teilhard's intellectual achievement is one of the first things that strikes one who picks up his major works. Many a reader has never gotten beyond the first chapters of *Phenomenon of Man* because of the intellectual demands it places upon him. Yet there is much more to Teilhard than his masterwork reveals. He was a man of the mind—that was his specialization, and the concrete work he did in the field, in writing his scholarly articles, and in his religious and philosophical books and essays, demonstrates that. He was a whole man, however, as we have insisted from the beginning, and the intellect played the role in his person that it plays in any healthy individual; it enabled him to pursue an effective life. His intellectual probings are marked by a passionate thrust toward the practical life of action.

If we look carefully, below the surface of Teilhard's argumentation in behalf of the ultimately personalizing character of reality, the essential trustworthiness of the life process, and the final victory of good, we can see how the entire train of thought presses from the realm of thought toward the realm of action. He discounts as models for understanding the nature of reality both the image of impersonality, as contained in the concept of "force" or "energy," and the image of entropy, the final disintegration of the world. These models are inconceivable, because they do not serve man as resources for conceiving a universe in which man is thoroughly at home. The reason why it is so important for Teilhard to be able to "think" the universe is precisely so that he can enable man to be *at home* in his world. To be at home implies possessing the resources for meaningful action. He wrote that "the Human, having become aware of its uncompleted state, cannot . . . give itself with passion" to any projected course of action that might seem appealing unless it can discern a consummation (FM, 277). This is the thrust of his Law of the Conservation of the Personal. Human life and action are the values which Teilhard seeks to serve with his intellectual formulations and his interpretation of the contemporary history through which he was living. And the significance of Christian faith lies in the fact that it points to the real consummation which is essential for that life and action.

In two striking pieces, one dating from Peking in 1943 and the other in 1945, Teilhard exhibits the fusion of the intellectual with human action, as well as the fusion of the human with the Christian. In the first essay, "Super-Humanity, Super-Christ, Super-Charity," he writes:

At this moment there are men, many men, who by making the conjunction of the two ideas of Incarnation and evolution a real element in their lives, are succeeding in effecting the synthesis of the personal and the universal. For the first time in history men have become capable not only of knowing and serving evolution but of *loving* it (SC, 172).

Knowing and acting are thus synthesized in the faith that Christ perfects evolution. He continues his reflection by observing that not only is the universe moving toward increasing organic complexity, but that this complexity takes place where *activity* is heightened. Truth, he writes, consists of coherence and "activance" or "activating potential" (defined as "the power an intellectual or mystical outlook possesses of developing spiritual energies in us and super-stimulating them") (SC, 171 n.). Coherence and "activance" were the criteria which Teilhard employed to establish the truth of his model of the personal as characterizing reality, as well as his insistence that life is reliable. *Intellectual theories provide a coherence which makes action possible, and their validity is tested by their ability to do so; the ultimate coherence for both theory and action is provided by Christ and Christian faith.* In this one sentence, we have summarized Teilhard's fundamental test of truth. And we must remember that "coherence" for him has two dimensions: internal consistency of one's total world view and congruity between that world view and the essence of human personhood.

The later essay, "Action and Activation," lays out this theme even more clearly. For the ancients, he says, "to be" was "to know," but for moderns, "to be" is "to grow" and "to become." He goes on, in a passage that is of highest significance for his entire vision:

> ... in relation to our will *the real must ... be, to the highest possible degree and with no limit, actable and activating.* In other words, there would be a contradiction, an ontological imbalance, in the world if our capacity to desire and to act were found to be greater, even in one single point, than the possibilities offered to us by our cosmic environment (SC, 174, italics added).

In practice, Teilhard asserted, the "first and essential condition of reality" is that it possess the ability to fulfill our "capacities and aspirations for understanding and creating .... What is the most intelligible and the most activating is necessarily the most real and the most true" (SC, 175).

These considerations throw a clearer light on Teilhard's explicit and implicit relations to several other movements of our time. First of all, the concern for action as a metaphysical principle that is essential for truth plainly sets Teilhard apart from all world-renouncing movements, whether those movements be religious or not. He himself considered this to be the chief difference between his own mysticism and the mysticism of the East, but he also rejected those ascetical interpretations of Christianity that withdrew from the world. Whether these movements urged withdrawal because of the world's uncleanness or because of a concern for contemplation, they cut the nerve of action.

Perhaps, even more interestingly, the concern for action helps us to interpret better Teilhard's stance in relation to Existentialism and Marxism. The thinking that lies behind the passages we have just quoted—especially the idea that "the real must be actable and activating"—bears a strong kinship to both of these other twentieth-century movements. Both Sartre and Camus, for example, were clear in their insistence that "to be" is "to grow" or "to act"—"existence (action) precedes being." The power of a Dr. Rieux in *The Plague* lies in his unflinching courage, in the face of an adversity which he could not comprehend, *to act* for the welfare of his fellow men. Although Teilhard interpreted Sisyphus as the epitome of the demoralized slave who has no incentive to meaningful action, Camus saw in his futile labors the conscious and courageous decision to act despite the apparent eternal meaninglessness of that action. Thus, according to Camus, the decisive moment for Sisyphus is when, after having pushed the stone up the mountainside, he sees it roll back down and turns to descend to the plain, where he will once again put his shoulder to the stone.

> It is during that return, that pause, that Sisyphus interests me . . . That hour like a breathing-space which returns as surely as his suffering, that is the hour of consciousness. At each of those moments when he leaves the heights and gradually sinks toward the lairs of the gods, he is superior to his fate. He is stronger than his rock . . . Sisyphus . . . knows the whole extent of his wretched condition: it is what he thinks of during his descent. The lucidity that was to constitute his torture at the same time crowns his victory.[5]

There is action, and there is self-awareness as an individual—both of them Teilhardian themes!

Similarly, the emphasis on action, the actable, and the activating is integral to Marxist philosophy. Roger Garaudy, in his dialogue with Christianity, *From Anathema to Dialogue*, remarks that at the very heart of Marxist thought stands the statement by Marx "that the object, reality, that we apprehend through our senses is understood . . . *as sensuous human activity.*"[6] Or, "the very spirit of Marxism is essentially *a methodology of historical initiative.*" Garaudy's comments are in harmony with the celebrated maxim by Marx: "the philosophers have only *interpreted* the world . . . the point, however, is to *change* it."[7]

Teilhard was aware of the affinities between his thought and Marxism. Robert Speaight presents a lucid summary of Teilhard's appreciation of the Marxist hope for a better world, its concern for energetic action in the world, and its unwillingness to turn aside from the earthiness of the physical environment. Strangely, as we have already observed, we do not find that same awareness of the kinship with the action-oriented philosophy of the Existentialists. This may be due to the Existentialist motifs of despair and hopelessness, since Teilhard considered these to be the most dangerous obstacles to man's future. Nevertheless, despite the kinship with the Existentialists and Marxists, Teilhard parted ways with them because their vision lacked what he considered to be the total coherence that would make human action meaningful and which would therefore make their vision *true*. He marked three components that belong together: coherence, activance, and truth. Existentialism and Marxism lacked coherence, in Teilhard's opinion, and therefore they did not qualify as truth. Existentialism posited a fundamental absurdity as the ultimate character of reality, as we have noted in Camus. Marxism posted an impersonal process. As Garaudy writes:

> Marxism asks the same questions as the Christian does, is influenced by the same exigency, lives under the same tension towards the future. The crucial factor is that Marxism does not . . . succumb to the temptation to affirm, behind the activity, a being who is its source . . . . My thirst does not prove the existence of the spring. For the Marxist, the infinite is absence and exigency, while for the Christian, it is promise and presence.[8]

The Marxist knows, says Garaudy, that alienation resides in the promise and affirmation of presence—that is, in answers that are illusory. Marxism rather affirms and takes command of pure exigency or risk. He goes on to say that the Marxist does not need to posit a God, a person, but rather only an absolute future as the ultimate. The Marxist needs no guarantees; he lives in risk, with only the confidence that he is acting as part of creation.[9] Teilhard would agree with Garaudy that it is not necessary to affirm "a being" behind the process of the world, but he would insist there is within the process an ultimate personalizing center that possesses power.

For Teilhard, both the absurdity of Camus and the absolute exigency and future process of Garaudy are inadequate, because they are not in closest consonance with the personality and centeredness that characterize the essence of human being. The result is that the ultimate in each vision is different from, contradictory to, and less than the essential being that man knows to be within himself. This is the point at which the coherence of the Existentialist and the Marxist break down. Consequently, Teilhard would say, in the long run, neither can sustain the action they both espouse. And since "the faith which finally triumphs must be the one which shows itself to be more capable than any other of inspiring Man to action," Christian faith must take pre-eminence over these other faiths as man's surest hope for fulfillment.

There are a number of considerations, however, that demand that we probe beneath the surface of the elegant consistency of Teilhard's system of thought. For one, we must ask the pragmatic question of whether Christian faith has *in fact* demonstrated that it can inspire men to action more successfully than other faiths. Teilhard himself spoke incisively about Christians who are indifferent to man and to human action, who are skeptics concerning man. He writes, rather epigram-matically, that it is one thing for Christians to suffer and die joyfully in order that the world might grow greater, but it is quite another thing for Christians to accept the death that comes because they are blocking mankind's road (SC, 150). He could, no doubt, sympathize with the exasperation of Garaudy, who complains, "We sometimes get the im-pression, if we compare the writings of Teilhard, Père Dubarle or Father Rahner with the so-called 'popular' publications, that two different religions are being taught under the same name."[10] It is not a simple thing to judge, over the centuries, what faiths have shown themselves most capable of inspiring man to action, but Teilhard has insisted, all the way through, that empirical, demonstrable evidence is the test—for his faith, as well as for others. The way in which one interprets the evidence concerning Christianity at this point will influence his attitude toward the cogency of Teilhard's argument. Teilhard really did not probe deeply the significance of the non-Christian visions that did suc-ceed in inspiring men to action even though they did not affirm the metaphysical assumption of a personalizing universe.

Secondly, we recognize that the fundamental incoherence of Marxism and Existentialism may be admitted, incoherence measured by Teilhard's twofold concept of coherence (after all, both Garaudy and Camus have spoken eloquently of their willingness to act courageously in man's behalf *without* the guarantees that the ultimate coherence of Teilhard's would provide), without granting that Teilhard's counter argument is satisfactory. In the final analysis, Teilhard's criterion of coherence, defined in his distinctive fashion, is sheer assertion. As such, it can be accounted for in a number of ways. It could be a manifestation of Teilhard's apparent psychological need for an absolute,[11] or it could be his application of the classical philosophical and theological methodology of the "analogy of being." The Marxist, the Existentialist, and the Freudian would suggest that Teilhard is projecting a personalizing reality, and that the projection is an illusion. Teilhard was sensitive to this charge. He knew that he was open to the accusation that he was engaging in anthropocentrism and projection. He denied, however, that anthropocentrism is necessarily either illusory or opposed to objectivity. In *Esquisse d' un univers personnel*, he calls the distinction between anthropocentrism and objectivity into question. *"La vérité de l'Homme est la vérité de l'Univers pour l'Homme, c'est à dire, la Vérité, tout simplement."* "The truth concerning man is man's truth concerning the universe, that is to say, very simply, it is *the* truth" (Oe, VI, VI, 71). Or, as Peter Berger has remarked recently, "To say that religion is a human projection does not logically preclude the possibility that the projected meanings may have an ultimate status independent of man."[12] A reflection upon man, or a projection of reality shaped by man, may be a reflection of a reality that embraces both man and his world. Truth concerning man may, indeed, be truth concerning the universe. Teilhard did not, however, give the proper technical philosophical attention to the question of how mind and language use projections or models and analogies.

Hand in hand with these questions goes a third consideration— namely, the role and nature of *hope* in man's existence. Camus all but jettisons any hope for man. Man acts courageously and in behalf of his fellow man simply because that is all there can be for human beings. The denial of hope contradicts the fundamental nature of the world, as well as man's nature, says Teilhard, since hope points to a future-orientation that is intrinsic to the world process. The Marxist is more ambiguous. On one level, he is full of hope, working for the success of the revolution and the implementation of its goals as the fulfillment of the process of history. On another level, a certain ultimate pessimism has entered Marxist thinking that parallels Existentialism. To the pessimist, Teilhard responds as he did to Sartre and Camus. To the hopeful Marxist he replies that hope is irrational except there be an ultimate personalizing center toward which the world process is tending—a God. This is no superficial rejoinder; as we noted in the last chapter, it has been taken up time and again by the generation that has succeeded Teilhard. There is a sense in which, for men who are concerned to live courageously, the hope based on impersonal process collapses, and one is faced with only two fundamental choices: *either* Camus' struggle without hope *or* Teilhard's struggle based on hope in a personalizing universe. The alternative to both Camus and Teilhard is revealed in Camus' haunting question: "Why not suicide?" Or, as Teilhard put it, every man must ask himself: "Is it better to Be than not to Be?" The philosophical dimensions of hope point us toward Teilhard's concept of "future," which we discuss in the final section of this chapter.

Once again, these observations do not demonstrate that Teilhard is more right or wrong, more adequate or inadequate, than his opponents. At the level at which they are questioning, there is no simplistic "right" or "wrong." It is important, however, to clarify the level on which Teilhard is carrying forward the debate, because his promise lies precisely in his ability to go to the heart of the matter and there to offer a vision of truth whose coherence not only makes meaningful human action possible but actually stimulates that action. With this general understanding of the place of Christian faith and action in Teilhard's vision, we turn to a more detailed discussion of several specific elements which undergird his call to action.

B. *The Divine Milieu*

What, very specifically, can one say about the individual life that is grasped by the vision that Teilhard has set forth?—the life that is persuaded of his interpretation of current history, suggesting that the world is caught up in the evolutionary movement of complexification, tending toward the end of ultrahominization, unification of mankind, and personalization in the ultimate centeredness of point Omega? In 1926, Teilhard set down in *The Divine Milieu* his basic ideas concerning the interior life. This book was never approved by the censor, but it did receive considerable distribution in unpublished and privately published forms. The title of the work gives the clue to its content. The individual Christian is aware of his every moment and his every action existing within the divine milieu—that is, within an environment which is divine and oriented upon God as center. "God reveals himself everywhere, beneath our groping efforts, *as a universal milieu*, only because he is the ultimate point upon which all realities converge" (DM, 114). (It is important to note here, for later reference, that, as the point on which all realities converge, God is ahead in the evolutionary process, and hence the universal milieu is a forward-moving reality.)

The work is a psychological description, in the sense that it describes the psyche of the individual believer. It could be called a phenomenology of the psychic life of the faithful Christian. It concentrates upon two dimensions of human life, that in which man is an agent, *acting upon* the world and other persons, and that in which man *is acted upon* by events and persons outside himself. Teilhard refers to these two dimensions as *activity* and *passivity*. Passivity, however, does not refer to the state of repose and contemplation, but rather to the condition in which a person is the object, rather than the agent, of actions. Both activity and passivity stand as components of the action-oriented life of man.

God is environment and center, because he is present to both of these dimensions and gives them focus and meaning. Human activity is caught up so totally in God that every human endeavor works to complete the world in Christ Jesus. Teilhard states this view of action in formal syllogistic style and also in adorational prayer. Syllogistically:

At the heart of our universe, each soul exists for God, in our Lord.

But all reality, even material reality, around each one of us, exists for our souls.

Hence, all sensible reality, around each one of us, exists, through our souls, for God in our Lord (DM, 56).

Prayerfully:

The more I examine myself, the more I discover this psychological truth: that no one lifts his little finger to the smallest task unless moved, however obscurely, by the conviction that he is contributing infinitesimally (at least indirectly) to the building of something definitive—that is to say, to your work, my God (DM, 55 f.).

This summarizes the interior sensitivity of the believing Christian—he knows that any and all of his actions are sanctified, so that they contribute to building God's world. Any and all actions? Yes, so long as man recognizes that his actions are not to focus on the world as such, to the extent that the world might bid him be less than he ought to be—as when he is tempted to bask in pride at his success, rest content with less than his best performance, or sink in despair.

From man's point of view, Teilhard observes, activity is the most important dimension of life, but in reality "the passive is immeasurably the wider and deeper part" (DM, 75). Man wrestles with the Angel, like Jacob, and after he has wrestled, he is brought to recognize that, in the final act that is to unite him to the All, the two terms of the union are utterly disproportionate. He, the lesser, has to receive rather than to give. He finds himself in the grip of what he thought he could grasp (DM, 74).

We think of the man Teilhard de Chardin, who suffered much from policies that others had formulated, when we read his description of the mystery and precariousness of human life, as it is lived under the rubric of passivity. He speaks of the passivities of growth as the two hands of God, one merged with our own inner self, so that our inner development is God's work, the other an external force that brings to bear upon us "the whole sum of the forces of the universe . . . to work in us the effect which God desires" (DM, 79). Christian resignation plays a powerful role in Teilhard's spirituality, a resignation that rests in the confidence that even the greatest evil will be transfigured by God. Failure, weakness, all will be transfigured, even though we cannot understand it. Teilhard's meditation on passivities that diminish us reaches its climax in his powerful reflection upon death:

> When the painful moment comes in which I suddenly awaken to the fact that I am ill or growing old; and above all at that last moment when I feel I am losing hold of myself and am absolutely passive within the hands of the great unknown forces that have formed me; in all those dark moments, O God, grant that I may understand that it is you (provided only my faith is strong enough) who are painfully parting the fibers of my being in order to penetrate to the very marrow of my substance and bear me away within yourself (DM, 89 f.).

Such emphasis on passivity and resignation would seem strange in light of what we have said about Teilhard's concern for action, if we did not remember that he is speaking of the passivity that coexists with activity in the Christian believer—the passivity and resignation of a man who never ceases to act, but who recognizes that activity includes setback, failure, weakness, and death, and that these are the consequences of forces we cannot control. Similarly, the Christian is at one and the same time the most attached to the world and the most ascetic in his detachment from it. Attachment and detachment are related as breathing in and breathing out. The logic of this relation is as follows: In order to be united with God,

> you must first of all *be*--be yourself as completely as possible. And so you must develop yourself and take possession of the world *in order*

to be. Once this has been accomplished, then is the time to think about renunciation; then is the time to accept diminishment for the sake of *being in another*. Such is the sole and twofold precept of complete Christian asceticism (DM, 96).

Or, to recall his more philosophical discussion, first one must be centered as a self (active, attached), and then one can understand what it means to enter into union with all others in socialization, accepting the sacrifices and compromises that union entails (passive, detached). The succession of "first" and "second" is not to be overemphasized; as with breathing in and breathing out, the two must go together.

The over-all impact of the spirituality that Teilhard embodied in his own life and reflected upon in *The Divine Milieu* is to set the individual Christian totally within the network or matrix of the physical world, participating in it totally, because it is his milieu, the womb in which he lives, the source of his very self. But this milieu or matrix is also divine, inasmuch as God is in its events, its physical stuff, and in its development; God is the center of meaning and the goal that animates the world. When man acts, he is contributing to God's work; when he passively reacts, he is reacting to God. To say, then, that the world is the milieu in which man lives at peace, as in a womb, is to say that he lives in God, as his matrix and his center. By relating God to both man's activities and his passivities, and by setting man at peace or at home in both, Teilhard has really covered all the possibilities; that is why it is proper to say that man is *totally* within the matrix of the world and therefore of the divine; he is giving and receiving, doing and suffering, within that matrix. Teilhard proposed the Christian spirituality set forth in *The Divine Milieu* as a style of life appropriate to the contemporary world view. It was a style suited to the scientifically oriented person, because it was world-affirming; it took the earthiness of the material world very seriously, was psychologically meaningful, and gave significance to work that was devoted to wordly ends. There is evidence that Teilhard made significant impact upon laymen to whom he gave this material in retreats and lectures.

In line with this practical spirituality, we can discern another theme of Teilhard's—namely, the need for the Christian to affirm his unity with matter. This theme permeates *The Divine Milieu*, as well as his other spiritual works. In "The Mass on the World," he relates every part of the liturgy of the Mass to God's presence in the material world and man's participation in that divinized world.

But you, my God, are the inmost depths, the stability of that eternal *milieu*, without duration or space, in which our cosmos emerges gradually into being and grows gradually to its final completeness . . . . Your creatures are not merely so linked together in solidarity that none can exist unless all the rest surround it, but all are so dependent on a single central reality that a true life, born in common by them all, gives them ultimately their consistence and their unity (HU, 21 f., 25).

One could, thus, use Teilhard's spiritual meditations and his understanding of the Church's sacraments as the clue to his entire theological thought. In them he sees the presence of God permeating the world and supporting his people, since they, too, are part of the world God has transfigured. In "The Spiritual Power of Matter," he pictures a swimmer who thrashes the water with his limbs as he swims, and Teilhard imagines that the swimmer and the power of the water are engaged in conflict. The water speaks to the swimmer:

Son of earth, steep yourself in the sea of matter, bathe in its fiery waters, for it is the source of your life and your thoughtfulness. You thought you could do without it because the power of thought has been kindled in you? You hoped that the more thoroughly you rejected the tangible, the closer you would be to spirit: that you would be more divine if you lived in the world of pure thought, or at least more angelic if you fled the corporeal? Well, you were like to have perished of hunger . . . Son of man, bathe yourself in the ocean of matter; plunge into it where it is deepest and most violent; struggle in its currents and drink of its waters. For it cradled you long ago in your preconscious existence; and it is that ocean that will raise you up to God . . . And then the frenzy of the battle gave place in his heart to an irresistible longing to *submit;* and in a flash he discovered, everywhere present around him, *the one thing necessary* (HU, 63 ff.).

C. The Cosmic Christ

Teilhard's twin themes, affirming the unity of man and matter and acknowledging that man's activities and passivities are fully accepted as part of God's activity, go hand in hand with his understanding of God's work as creator and Christ's work as incarnate Lord. God and Christ are in the process that Teilhard interpreted under the category of complexification, and they are in the historical events that he illumined thereby.

We recall that Teilhard wished to speak of the world and its history in terms that were dynamic rather than static, in terms of *development*, and that he added the suffix "genesis" to certain words to denote this development. One could even say that he attempted to reinterpret the Christian faith in terms of "genesis." Three days before he died, Teilhard wrote a sketch of his thought, the last page in his journal, which suggests the process comprised of the following terms: Cosmos= Cosmogenesis—Biogenesis—Noogenesis—Christogenesis. He based this thinking on a number of passages from St. Paul, including I Corinthians 15:26–28: Christ rules "that God may be all in all." This concept has been designated in the theological tradition as the "cosmic Christ," because it interprets the Incarnation to refer to God's union with matter in Christ, with Christ's power and meaning unfolding within the development of the physical world, giving it meaning and direction.

We must keep in mind Teilhard's theory of creation as creative union, as we referred to it in the previous chapter in the discussion of evil. Teilhard holds that God called into being a void or nothingness which has no existence at all except through the unitive process by which God orders and arranges it. This process of ordering results in a movement toward the unification of all that emerges from the void; the entire process counts as creation, since it is the ordering and uniting that gives reality to the constituents of the process. Creation aims at union, because the void is a "multiple"—that is, a plurality requiring meaning and order. Georges Crespy suggests that we understand Teilhard's theory more clearly if we keep in mind the Einsteinian insight that mass equals energy. We normally think of creation in terms of mass or substance, but Teilhard is suggesting, says Crespy, that the very process or energy of ordering the void constitutes the creation.[13]

Teilhard elaborates the place of Christ in this process of creative union in three essays that are collected in the volume *Science and Christ:* "Note on the Universal Christ" (1920), "Science and Christ" (1921), and "My Universe" (1924). Christ is the center and the synthesizing force of the process which forms the world.

> By the Universal Christ, I mean Christ the organic center of the entire universe . . . that is to say, the center not only of moral and religious effort, but also of all that that effort implies—in other words of all physical and spiritual growth (SC, 14).

In the 1924 essay, Teilhard closes a paragraph on the universal Christ with the words, "That, then, will suffice to make my theological position clear" (SC, 56). The paragraph asserts, "This is the point we must bear in mind: in no case could the cosmos be conceived, and realized, without a supreme center of spiritual consistence" (SC, 56). Christ is this center of spiritual consistence, and therefore he is identical to the Omega point toward which the unitive creation process tends. At several points, Teilhard symbolizes his meaning by referring to a cone:

> One could say that the structure of things, taken individually or as a whole, *is similar to that of a cone*. A cone has an apex and a base, a center of convergence and a zone of indefinite divergence. An observer who follows the axis of a cone as he proceeds towards the apex, finally reaches the point where all the generating lines meet and join up. A reversal of direction leads him towards an endless dissociation of the elements that make up the figure (SC, 30).

If we wish to probe to the inner core, the essence, of the world, we ought not push "towards what lies *deepest below or furthest behind but towards what is most interior in the soul and most new in the future*" (SC, 30). The process of unitive creation pushes toward the interior and forward line of the cone's apex. That line is also the line of the Omega point and the line of the Christ who is the centering and synthesizing force of the world process. When we think of how central the complexifying process of unitive creation and the Omega point of that process are to Teilhard's vision, we can grasp the pertinence of the comment that several students of Teilhard have made, that his entire theology is a Christology, or more exactly, a "cosmo-Christology."[14]

If Christ does coincide with the Omega, then "the grandest and most necessary attribute we can ascribe to him is that of exerting a supreme physical influence on every cosmic reality without exception" (SC, 56 f.). The universe is "physically impregnated to the very core of its matter" by his influence. Christ, in other words, epitomizes the meaning and destiny of all reality, and as such is present throughout the material realm. In an analogous way, one would say that the axis and apex of the cone are present throughout the cone, since the "coneness" of every part of the cone depends upon the axis and apex. The reader will remember that this was true of the Omega point, as well; Omega is ahead, as the axis on which the world process of complexification is moving forward, but it is also present to every moment of that process.

This line of thinking results in a "physical intensity of grace," because Christ *is* the essence of the evolutionary world process in which man himself participates.

> By Baptism in cosmic matter and the sacramental water we are more
> Christ than we are ourselves—and it is precisely in virtue of this
> predominance in us of Christ that we can hope one day to be fully
> ourselves (SC, 58).

This intimate identification of Christ, grace, and the evolutionary process seems excessive, if not offensive, if we fail to remember that
Teilhard's theory of original sin conceives evil as a by-product of, and
obstacle to, the *process* of unification and not as an attribute of matter
itself. The intensity of grace in the world process serves as the basis for
Teilhard's assertion that the world is already "Christified" and is
capable of being rendered even more fully "Christic." The intention of
this concept of Christification, which may otherwise seem pretentious,
is to express Teilhard's fundamental vision that the destiny of the world
is summed up in Christ—once again, the analogy of the cone may be
helpful, inasmuch as, without axis and apex, it would be senseless to
speak of the meaning of a cone at all, and thus the entire cone is
"apex-ified."

Teilhard set his cosmic Christ in sharp opposition to what he termed
the "juridical" interpretation of Christ, which had dominated the history of the Church so as to leave the Pauline cosmic emphasis stag-
nated. He despaired of ever convincing his juridically oriented
opponents; he writes; "I have, in fact, become convinced that men
include two irreconcilable types of minds: the physicalists (who are
'mystics') and the juridicists" (SC, 55). Juridical categories are
"simpler, safer, and more convenient" for expressing the relations between God and man, in that they lend themselves to family and other
interpersonal images.

> Such analogies are true, in as much as union in Christ is effected
> between persons, but they are incomplete. If we are to express the
> whole truth we must correct them by analogies drawn from realities
> that are specifically *natural* and *physical*. The friendship of God and
> adoption by God are expressions that include an adaptation of the
> universe, a transformation, a recasting, that are organic and cannot
> be cancelled (SC, 18 f.).

Since juridical or personal categories have in fact dominated most of
the Church's description of Christ's work, and since these categories
seem irreplaceable for dealing with the realities of guilt, reconciliation,
and justification, it is important to note that Teilhard is arguing primarily against a view that would overlook their incompleteness. He

does not mean to reject personal images of Christ's work. Concerned as he is for the totality of the world process within which religious realities take place, he is determined to deal with the organic, physical implications of Christ.

If Christ is to function in fact as center and unifier of the world process, he must become a part of it. The cosmic Christ cannot remain in the realm of abstract principle; the world process which he transforms is by definition concrete. The historical Jesus of Nazareth, in other words, cannot be obscured by the Christ who is Omega. Furthermore, his character as Omega does not cancel out his suffering and death, since unifying and giving purpose to the multiple that emerges from the original void is precisely the most difficult thing of all to accomplish and the point at which evil arises. "That is why the Incarnation of the Word was infinitely painful and mortifying—so much so that it can be symbolized by a cross" (SC, 60). Teilhard describes movingly his conviction that the aeons prior to Jesus' birth were necessary in order for the process of complexification to prepare itself for the entry of the Omega into the process of matter. As for the Incarnation itself, "The Redeemer could penetrate the stuff of the cosmos, could pour himself into the life-blood of the universe, only by first dissolving himself in matter, later to be reborn from it" (SC, 60). The suffering and death of Jesus amount to the actual assimilation of human life, an inescapable requisite for him if he were really to conquer as Lord. Death was necessary if the disparate elements that resisted unification were to be brought together and their unifier were to be united indissolubly with them. The resurrection stands as a cosmic event, in which Christ assumed his function as the universal center. In Jesus, the Omega has united itself with the world process which it directs, participated fully in the dynamics of that process and shared the pain of the unitive thrust, and then finally risen to effective power over the process.

The place of the Catholic Church rests on the fact that in it the influence of the cosmic Christ is transmitted, chiefly through the Eucharist and Christian action. There is a sense in which the Church is the prolongation of the axis and apex of the cone, of the Omega. Since the entire world is Christifiable and capable of even fuller Christification, the identity of the Church epitomizes the meaning of the world in a way analogous to that in which Christ does. When Teilhard said Mass, he tells us, he imagined that the entire world was the bread, the

Host that Christ was offering up to God. Christ cannot be confined to the elements of bread and wine.

> Since he is above all omega, that is, the universal "form" of the world, he can attain his organic balance and plenitude only by mystically assimilating . . . all that surrounds him. The Host is like a blazing hearth from which flames spread their radiance. Just as the spark that falls into the heather is soon surrounded by a wide circle of fire, so, in the course of centuries, the sacramental Host . . . is continually being encircled more closely by another, infinitely larger, Host, which is nothing less than the universe itself—the universe gradually being absorbed by the universal element. Thus when the phrase "This is my body" is pronounced, "this" means first of all the bread; but secondarily, in a second phase occurring in nature, the matter of the sacrament is the world, throughout which there spreads, so to complete itself, the superhuman presence of the universal Christ. The world is the final, and the real, Host into which Christ gradually descends, until his time is fulfilled (SC, 65).

Here Teilhard's Christian identity comes through with characteristic clarity. This identity, however, as we have already suggested in referring to Teilhard's Christian humanism, is allied to the universally human, as its fulfillment, and in a sense its Omega. In the next section, we will indicate how this view of the Church and its identity serves as a strong stimulus for action in the world.

Even this brief sketch of Teilhard's doctrine of Christ serves to suggest the power and mystical insight of his vision. Vigorous theological debate has opened him up to several important criticisms. The Protestant theologian misses a careful attention to the results of modern historical investigations of the New Testament. Teilhard's picture of Jesus Christ seems excessively metaphysical and dogmatic when compared to the meticulous critical studies that have been done on Jesus' actual person and activity. The impersonality that inevitably attends the cosmic and physical emphasis in Teilhard's picture of Christ has been singled out for its possible obscuring of the personal and existential impact of Christ's redemptive work. There is clearly much work yet to be done in assimilating the motif of the cosmic Christ and relating it properly to the more conventional personal motifs of Christian theology, but the promise of Teilhard's stimulus makes his contribution to the understanding of Christ a very great one.[15]

D. Building the Earth

Although Teilhard's understanding of the cosmic Christ who is Omega of the world process and his sacramental intensifying of the relation between Christ and matter bear the marks of mystical vision, they carry also immense significance for human action. If the entire world is the body of Christ and if "we are more Christ than we are ourselves," the action that takes place within this milieu of divine presence is charged with theological significance at every point, even when it is but the work of a little finger. Teilhard's spirituality is, as we have already indicated, fully oriented toward a life of action. We have hinted, however, that there is some ambiguity in Teilhard's spur to action. Some of the directives he gives could lead more to complacency than to aggressive activity. Consider his confidence that man's passivities are to be trusted, that the actions we suffer from others and from the world will not ultimately destroy but will be transfigured by God into good. Even the failures of the active person will become part of the final victory. Is this not an invitation to take the struggle less seriously than one might otherwise? If even failure is to be transfigured, why be anxious for victory, for reaching the goal? Teilhard exhibits here a confidence in the providence of God, guiding all things and events, that has in fact been used in the past by some religious groups as a reason to withdraw from active concern for changing the world, as a reason for retreating into contemplation and asceticism that are far removed from the principles of actability and activance. Similarly, if God through Christ is incarnate within the evolutionary process, of what use is human action? Would it not seem more plausible for man to ride the current of the process, so to speak, completely passive, so that he could be assured of reaching the consummation of the evolutionary progression?

Teilhard himself did not derive such directives from these doctrines but, on the contrary, drew the conclusion that human action was an ethical urgency and a philosophical absolute. As the title for this chapter we have chosen one of Teilhard's exhortations dating from 1950, in an essay dealing with the "Probable Coming of an Ultra-Humanity":

> Clearly, in light of what I have said, we have no grounds for expecting any relaxation, still less any end, of the process of compressive socialization which has now begun; and this being so it is

fruitless to seek to escape the whirlwind that is closing in on us. What is of extreme importance, on the other hand, is that we should know what course to steer, and *how we must spiritually conduct ourselves if we are to ensure that the totalitarian embrace which enfolds us will have the effect, not of de-humanizing us through mechanization, but (as seems possible) of super-humanizing us by the intensification of our powers of understanding and love* (FM, 276, italics added).

Have we here come upon one of the undigestible problems in Teilhard's thought that he bequeathed to us unresolved? Intellectually and theologically, the answer must be "Yes." He is not the first theologian or philosopher to be burdened with this particular tension between the determinism of a providential God and the freedom of a humanity that must act if it is to survive. His emphasis upon divine providence threatens to cut the nerve of human activity, whereas the raising of that activity to philosophical and religious primacy opens up the thorny question of whether God grows and suffers, as a result of his involvement in the process of complexification (see SC, Chapter II).

For Teilhard, this dilemma did not seem an urgent one, because he obviously presupposed from the very beginning that human beings within the evolutionary process are acting creatures. Complacency, withdrawal, and despair are to him *secondary* aspects of the process of life, minor themes when compared with the dominant theme. They are nonetheless real, and he recognizes that they may indeed become dominant and destroy man (here again, the contradiction—how could they become dominant without destroying God, also?). Nevertheless, they are the deviation, the by-product, the unnatural, in contrast with the natural condition of aggressive action. Passivities and resignation are events within the larger context of action—much like the Marxist conviction that the "revolution" is a lifelong enterprise, within which setbacks are temporary "learning experiences." The revolutionary does not lessen his efforts, since revolution is the "natural" condition; complacency, the unnatural deviation. For Teilhard, the evolutionary, complexifying process *is* a process comprised of acting persons.

Teilhard believed that the process of complexification "directs itself to those areas and that state in which activity is constantly heightened" (SC, 172). The unification of mankind, leading to the ultimate unification or convergence in point Omega, is an intellectual unity, to be sure, but it is above all *a unity that is attained through action*. This is why, to use one of Teilhard's most popular and influential terms, the

Christian must be actively engaged in "world-building." Christians have always known, he says, that we draw nearer to God when we love our neighbor, but what we have not recognized is that it is impossible

> to love either God or our neighbor without assisting the progress, in its physical entirety, of the terrestrial synthesis of the spirit: since it is precisely the progress of this synthesis which enables us to draw closer together among ourselves, while at the same time it raises us towards God. Because we love, and in order that we may love even more, we find ourselves happily and especially compelled to participate in all the endeavors, all the anxieties, all the aspirations and also all the affections of the earth—*insofar as these embody a principle of ascension and synthesis* (FM, 95).

Or, to put it in terms of the cosmic Christology:

> Human action can be related to Christ, and can co-operate in fulfillment of Christ, not only by the intention, the fidelity, and the obedience in which . . . it is clothed, but also by the actual *material content* of the work done. All progress, whether in organic life or in scientific knowledge, in aesthetic faculties or in social consciousness, can therefore be made Christian even in its object (SC, 17).

These quotations contain what is perhaps the most dynamic and "new" thrust in all of contemporary Christianity—and its relevance is not limited to Christians. Teilhard, of course, is not the only contemporary Christian who has enunciated a doctrine of world-building, but few have been able to place this wisdom in the broad context of cosmic evolution and human history. This motif of "building the earth" has renovated Christian spirituality and practical life whereever Teilhard has had an influence, because of its insistence that it is only in such activity that we can love either God or our neighbor. And although there are warrants for this insight in Scripture and in the Christian tradition, there is a freshness and novelty in this desire to equate earth-building with God's design and will. Teilhard does include his criterion for such efforts, italicized in the foregoing quotation: they must be activities that work for unity and synthesis, contributing to the process of complexification.

The motif of earth-building is one of the points where Teilhard's vision has established contact with the emergence of what is called "secular Christianity," the interpretation of the Christian faith that calls for involvement in the activities of the world for the sake of God. When we reflect on this secularizing dimension of Teilhard's thought, we touch another area in which he holds promise for us today. One of the chief difficulties with the strategies for "secular Christianity" that have been proposed today—by Dietrich Bonhoeffer, Harvey Cox, the so-called "Christian atheists," and other "radical" Christians—is that they have had difficulty in holding their secularity and their Christian identity together. In their own persons, the two have lived side by side, to be sure, but they have not always developed an effective total synthesis of the two. For some, this is no problem; there are those who are willing to preserve their Christianness at all costs, in spite of great ethical and psychic contradiction, even if it means that their faith is irrelevant to the worldly lives that most people must live; others are fully prepared to jettison their Christian identity, convinced that commitment to fundamental human values is goal enough and consolation enough for this life. For either of these groups, each of which is able to fashion a stance in life by collapsing either the secular or the Christian pole and embracing what remains, "secular Christianity" is no problem. The peace that these groups have gained, however, is at the expense of integrity—or at least it is a new kind of integrity that has cut off either the world or Christian identity.

For those whose integrity demands Christianness and worldliness together in equilibrium, Teilhard holds considerable promise. There is no question but that his vision promoted commitment to the building of the earth—that much is a fact, perceptible both in his own person and in those who have been influenced by him. It is also beyond doubt that his vision conveys a thoroughly Christian identity—even if it is an identity that is questioned by some Christians. His adamant refusal to leave either his order or the Church when he was persecuted by them and his refusal to "lose" himself in a predominantly secular group of colleagues in China and America testify to the power of his Christian identity. What enabled him to hold the two together so organically in synthesis were (1) the magnitude of his humanism; (2) the depth of his interpretation of the Incarnation of Jesus Christ and its cosmic, material implications; and (3) the fullness of his intellectual synthesis—ranging from theology through metaphysics and science, the total synthesis pushing relentlessly through to concrete embodiment in action and personal spirituality.

We do not overlook the vulnerability of his intellectual synthesis at points. We have discussed the problematic character of Teilhard's scholarly judgments and of his assumptions concerning the personal model as a basis for interpreting reality. We have surveyed the inner tensions between his conviction concerning God's providence and the need for human initiatives. We have also called attention to his personal anxieties and doubts—at times his religious faith *did* falter. We have no desire to cloud the "real" Teilhard with the smoke of a devotee's incense. Nevertheless, even with the problematic aspects of his work in mind—or should we say, *especially* when we hold those reservations in —Teilhard looms before us as a monumental Christian humanist whose intellectual synthesis is so broad that it staggers the mind. Only the great thinkers of our time have matched the breadth of this synthesis: men like Whitehead, Toynbee, and Heidegger. But few of those who have matched (or surpassed) his intellectual synthesis have pushed out into the area of life and spirituality as he did. There are works as great or greater than *The Phenomenon of Man* (one thinks of Whitehead's *Process and Reality*, Heidegger's *Being and Time*, and Barth's *Epistle to the Romans*) that have appeared in the last half century; there are some works pertaining to the practical life that equal or surpass *The Divine Milieu* (the works of Mao, Gandhi, Freud). One would be hard put to find the name of one who has produced works that pertain to both the mind and the will in the way that Teilhard's have. Whether Teilhard can find an equal or not, however, is not the question. His promise lies in his synthesis of secularity and Christian meaning, a synthesis that owes its power to the quality of his intellectual vision, on the one hand, and to the force of his Christian humanism, on the other.

E. The Upward and the Forward—God and the World

It is simply a variation on the themes we have discussed thus far in this chapter to call attention to Teilhard's analysis of the relationship between the essence of secularity and Christian faith in terms of the Above and the Ahead (*en avant*), the Upward and the Forward. We must keep in mind that Teilhard rejected static conceptualities in his vision of the process of evolving complexification. He saw the essence of the secular world view to be that of faith in the Ahead, the conviction that the forward movement of the world process would bring a satisfactory consummation with it (note how accurately this describes Garaudy's Marxism). This stands in contrast with the religious world view of the past—whether Christian or some other religious perspective—that located the consummation in the Above and thus sought only an upward movement, out of the world.

> The Higher Life, the Union, the long dreamed-of consummation that has hitherto been sought *Above*, in the direction of some kind of transcendency: should we not rather look for it *Ahead*, in the prolongation of the inherent forces of evolution? Above or ahead—or both? . . .
>
> This is the question that must be forced upon every human conscience by our increasing awareness of the tide of anthropogenesis on which we are borne. It is, I am convinced, the vital question, and the fact that we have thus far left it unconfronted is the root cause of all our religious troubles; whereas an answer to it, which is perfectly possible, would mark a decisive advance on the part of Mankind towards God. That is the heart of the problem (FM, 263).

This is what Teilhard calls "The problem of two faiths," the faith in the Above corresponding to classical Christianity, the faith in the Ahead to humanism. There is no health unless the two are understood to be, not in opposition, but rather one—they are "the two essential components of a complete humano-Christian mysticism" (SC, 203). As we have already discovered, the faith that focused exclusively on the Above is defective, because it does not take seriously the development of the world and the cosmic implications of the Incarnation. The faith in the Ahead is also inadequate by itself, however. We have not mentioned up to this point Teilhard's insistence on God's transcendence, but it is an important theme in his thought. As concerned as he was for the development of the world and "bathing" in the sea of matter, he did not believe that the world could fulfill itself or provide its own consummation. Rather, the evolutionary process points beyond itself to a transcendence. Teilhard does not adequately relate these two emphases in his intellectual synthesis, but it is clear that he held them together in his own mind, in tension though they might be. In other words, the ultimate personalizing and converging center, point Omega, is not a product of the material realm by itself, even though the process of material evolution possesses the intrinsic thrust toward Omega.

It is important for us to note that, in Teilhard's opinion, the forward thrust of the world process of complexification raises the question of God and gives shape to his conceptuality of God. The last paragraph of *Man's Place in Nature* is instructive at this point. The book is significant for Teilhard, in that it is his last full-scale summary of his theory of the world's development and man's place within it. Written in 1949, it is a kind of condensation of *The Phenomenon of Man*. At the very end of the book, after he has surveyed the process of complexification, closing with two chapters on the nature of the noosphere, he writes (and we follow George Shriver's translation):

> And it is at this point, if I am not mistaken, that into the science of evolution (in order that evolution may show itself capable of functioning in a hominized milieu) the problem of God is inserted—a God who is the Mover, Collector, Consolidator, and the God-Forward of evolution.[16]

Although he did not spell it out in great detail, this conception of God the "Mover, Collector, Consolidator, and God-Forward of evolution" is one of his theologically most promising contributions. In our discussion of the divine milieu, we mentioned only in passing that the all-embracing matrix of divine presence is fundamentally a forward-moving ambience. It would be a mistake to interpret Teilhard's comments about the milieu as a traditional mystical vision of an all-embracing present moment. His commitment to the conceptuality of evolutionary process makes such a static, present-oriented view impossible. Furthermore, Teilhard was really suggesting a fundamental revision of human and Christian perspectives, by pointing away from *beginnings* as the key to understanding reality toward the future as the key. The Christian tradition has for the most part followed the principle that God's purpose and will are discerned by looking at the past, to the origins of the world and our Christian religion. Teilhard suggests that the study of the past is "as empty of mystery as the geographical bowels of the continents . . . . It is a *mirage* that causes us to see the nature of things in their *origin* ("origins" recede before us incessantly like the *horizon*)" (SC, 30 f.).

Teilhard's insight that the thrust of the process of cosmic evolution and human history compel us to consider the Ahead as the key to meaning has borne fruit in recent years in the increasing attention that theologians and philosophers are giving the concept of the *future*. In part, they are motivated by a concern for the revolutionary movements of our day. Their reflections have led to the conclusion that revolution and rapid cultural change make little sense unless the future toward which such tendencies point is of fundamental metaphysical significance. The full implications of this effort to give metaphysical priority

[111]

to the future are not yet clear. It could entail a reversal of our traditional understanding of the future as a product of the past, or of events as the effects of prior causes. Once again, Teilhard's example of the cone comes to mind. It is the future or final condition of the cone, the apex toward which its axis moves and which gathers together all its lines of movement, that makes the cone what it is. At the present time, such talk is appealing, yet intellectually somewhat bewildering. It was Teilhard's conviction, however, that no conception of God and the Christian faith is adequate unless it includes futurism as fundamental component.

The concept of God-Forward serves also as an occasion for Teilhard to express his thoroughgoing Christian humanism. The Christian faith cannot possibly attain the Above except in and through the Forward movement toward the Ahead. Teilhard writes especially eloquently on this theme, and it is tempting to let him speak for himself:

> There can be no truly live Christian faith if it does not reach and raise up, in its ascending movement, the totality of mankind's spiritual dynamism. . . . Nor is faith in man psychologically possible if the evolutionary future of the world does not meet, in the transcendent, some focal point of irreversible personalization. In short, it is impossible to rise Above without moving Ahead, or to progress Ahead without steering towards the Above (SC, 203).

The Church's function, Teilhard writes, is to "Christianize all that is human in Man," but too often ecclesiastical authority condemns the human, and he fears that

> This authority, which is no more nor less than Christianity, will lose, to the extent that it fails to embrace as it should *everything that is human on earth*, the keen edge of its vitality and its full power to attract. Being for the time *incompletely human* it will no longer fully satisfy even its own disciples (FM, 265).

Therefore, the church can look forward only to defection and the de-Christianizing of the world if it does not recognize that the Above lies in the Ahead.

> The super-naturalizing Christian Upward is incorporated (not immersed) in the human Forward! And at the same time Faith in God, in the very degree in which it assimilates and sublimates within its own spirit the spirit of Faith in the World, regains all its power to attract and convert! . . . let there be revealed to us the possibility of

[112]

believing *at the same time and wholly* in God *and* the World, the one through the other (FM, 268 f.).

But in complete consistency with his insistence on concrete action, he writes:

> We must, however, be careful to note one thing: this dialectical demonstration that the "two faiths" can be reconciled, brilliant though it is, will inevitably remain without fruit so long as it is not offered to the world as something lived in practice. That theoretically, *in abstracto*, the Above and the Ahead of the universe should coincide, is all to the good, and even counts for a great deal. But if the solution proposed is to be truly convincing and *communicate itself as such*, it still has to make itself unmistakably recognizable—it must prove itself, in act and in reality ... what we need is not treatises or books, but men who will serve as examples ... men who are all the more convinced of the sacred value of human effort in that they are primarily interested in God (SC, 203 f.).

These sentiments moved Teilhard to defend staunchly the vocation of scientist-priests and worker-priests. The Church's unwillingness to give wholehearted support to the latter was a matter of great concern to him. The last essay that he wrote, during the month before he died, March, 1955, "Research, Work and Worship," included a defense of the worker-priest movement, and it presents a compact embodiment of his integrated concern for the Above, the Ahead, and the action that can serve man's ultimate superhumanizing. He begins the essay with a poignant recollection that throughout his life, ecclesiastical authority advised (and warned) him, "Go quietly ahead with your scientific work without getting involved in philosophy or theology." Fearing that the same advice would be given to young men today, he speaks to those "brilliant youngsters" who are now entering upon scientific careers. Concerning the advice he received, he writes, "I should like to remark to those it properly concerns that it is psychologically unviable and, what is more, directly opposed to the greater glory of God" (SC, 214). In the final paragraphs of this piece, he points to the inadequacies of St. Ignatius' *Spiritual Exercises*, their static motifs and their lack of awareness of the power of the Ahead. Finally, he writes, we must raise up scientist-priests, worker-priests, and workers of every type. We must provide them with the "right to tell themselves that they meet and consummate the Total Christ directly, *by working*" (SC, 219 f.). This will entail a revision of doctrine and Christian spiritual life, a new theological education for scientist-priests and worker-priests, but we need even more "a new and higher form of worship to be gradually disclosed by Christian thought and prayer, adapted to the needs of all of tomorrow's believers without exception" (SC, 220). This was the final full expression of his vision that Teilhard wrote for publication. It is a fitting close to our own study of the man.

Epilogue: The Promise of Teilhard

Throughout our study of Teilhard, we have symbolized his promise for us and our generation in the term *"Christian humanism."* In so doing, we have pushed back to a dimension of the classical Christian tradition, which understood that the use of the word "humanism" does not dilute or distort the adjective "Christian," but that rather the term "Christian humanism" indicates that Christian faith and life find their cutting edge in the pursuit of the most adequate forms of human existence. The Christian faith that sustained Teilhard found its strongest focus when it was concentrated on the great questions that confront Everyman in the twentieth century, and it reached its greatest intensity when it was struggling for the meaning that all sensitive men seek.

We have placed Teilhard in context by contrasting his thought and his quest with other contemporary forms of the human quest for meaning, precisely because his promise lies not so much in that he provided answers that still stand, but rather in that he put his questions in forms that still shape the human quest today. He asked: What is man's essential nature? What must man assume, if he is to survive as a human being? Must he assume that the process of life itself is a trustworthy matrix for his existence, that will not destory him or drive him mad? That there is a basic congruity between himself and the world? That the processes of his perception and thought are reliable? That he has a hope? That he must, if he is to survive as man, attend to his intimate relatedness to the support systems that Earth has provided for him? And that he must, at long last, take stock of himself as a mature, planetary animal whose existence henceforth will take place in one global society? In the years since he began his work, these questions have become even more pertinent, and Teilhard's relentless insistence that these questions belong together seems all the more obvious. That this is so may be clearer if we summarize briefly the various forms of the questions that Teilhard posed and the lines of thought that those questions still suggest for us.

1. In spite of his nonprofessional education and interest in the social sciences, particularly political science and sociology, he has proved to be visionary in his insight that the problem of relating collectivist and individualist tendencies in our social life is crucial for the future of man in the twentieth century. Furthermore, his insistence that *both* of these tendencies must be intensified, that neither can be collapsed in favor of the other, is still provocative for current efforts to understand and direct the progress of our common life.

2. The ecological thrust of Teilhard's thinking gives it a dimension that only now has assumed articulate force in men's minds. Every aspect of Teilhard's thought and meditation is permeated by the awareness that man lives in unity with and dependence upon the natural systems that surround him on his planet and in his universe. Therefore, when he asked the question of human survival as a species,when he projected his political speculation, and when he probed his religious faith, he did so with an ecological awareness that gives even his less sophisticated thought a striking relevance for us. His mature thought opens possibilities for us to move toward the resolution of problems that we now see as clearly as he did, because our existence is threatened by the disruption of our ecological balance. The issues of global planning, care for the natural environment, and man's unity with nature—issues that have just begun to permeate the general consciousness of our time—are issues that Teilhard learned to handle easily, and therefore he can be a useful guide for us.

3. Teilhard saw clearly that the questions that are most pressing for man will yield only to an effort that fully synthesizes intellectual probing and moral commitment. His peculiar mixture of mystical vision, scientific research, and philosophical probing is now the very style that seems most relevant to an age that is weary of the empty games that intellectuals like to play and frightened of the moral commitment of men who refuse to be guided by reason.

Teilhard understood that for Christians the chief theological problem posed by the post-modern era was that of conceiving in a new way the presence of God in the world. His theories of creation, evil, God-Forward and God-Above and the cosmic Christ were not only ahead of his own generation, but they still stand as markers for what is largely unexplored territory for theologians today. Teilhard's vision for

[116]

theology is all the more impressive when we consider that he was not a professional theologian and that the theories just mentioned are all rather sketchy and undeveloped.

But Christians, who might be expected to welcome Teilhard more eagerly than their non-Christian colleagues, have rather found him more disquieting, because his fully integrated vision, thoroughly marked as it is by the scientific and post-modern ethos, demands a redirecting of the Christian tradition that is very painful for the established churches and their theologians. Georges Crespy has spoken instructively about Teilhard's passionate conviction that his own vision would be fully at home in traditional Christian dogmatic structures, if those structures were only slightly "corrected." In this, Crespy observed, Teilhard was guilty of a grave error in judgment.

> We must also say rather openly that the theological outlines and plans of Teilhard as such are practically unsalvageable. They have been pursued within a conceptual framework which was not made for them and could not support them without some kind of difficulty . . . . [His efforts] in no way attest . . . to the solidity and firmness of traditional statements. On the contrary, they *correctly* testify in favor of an even more radical revision, no longer on the level with the statements, but on the deeper level of the fundamental understanding of the dogmatic equipment which we have inherited.[1]

By now, one wing of Christianity has clearly affirmed that the revision must be underway—a revision that grows, not out of a disregard or disdain for the catholic tradition of the Christian faith, but rather out of a respect and faith in that tradition, just as Teilhard's efforts were engendered by his very faith and obedience to his Church and to his order. But another wing of Christianity is reluctant to acknowledge that revisions are in order. It is this wing that still needs the apologetic footnotes in Teilhard's works, to be lulled by a false assurance that the new is not really new.[2] This wing is still offended by the term "Christian humanist," because it suspects that the two words that comprise it—Christian and humanist—are antithetical. For this group, Teilhard's injunctions that evangelizing and mission are synonymous with humanizing (now accepted by many church agencies and taught in seminaries) are simply signs of capitulating to the secular spirit.

The promise of Teilhard for the churches, therefore, is a challenge whose future is not fully certain. In terms of *practice*, it is the vision that the exercise of the Christian faith—love for God and for neighbor

—is earth-building, and this may be the most decisive innovation that confronts Christianity in our time. *Intellectually*, the challenge is conceptualizing the belief that God is intrinsic within the process of evolution and that Christ is at the very core of the movement of the world process toward its final destiny. Teilhard's vision produced an intellectual understanding of the Christian faith that was fully permeated by the scientific world view, as well as a pattern for Christian life that was informed by that same world view. Despite the decades of work by a few theologians and churchmen, it is still true that, by and large, the churches have internalized the scientific world view neither in their intellectual interpretation of the faith nor in the pattern of their practical life. On both counts—intellectual and practical—the churches are still overwhelmingly prescientific in their attitudes. There are signs that Teilhard's vision points to the way that the churches must eventually go. In 1969, twenty-five years after Teilhard was censored for revising the dogma of original sin, two books (one by a Protestant, one by a Catholic) that attempted the same revision, for many of the same reasons, were widely acclaimed as harbingers of the future!

Teilhard's promise as a resource for the churches lies in the fact that he held the spirit of radical revision together with an unabashed and unmistakable Christian identity. His was not a "secular" religion that seemed to be a warmed-over unbelief. On the contrary, his radicalism included obedience, public affirmation of God and traditional doctrine, participation in liturgy and sacraments, deep piety. Consequently, his radicalism is a viable option for those who would remain both human *and* Christian.

Teilhard's influence and promise will grow as men inside and outside the churches happily discover that Teilhard is a fellow traveler and a fellow seeker in their efforts to probe areas and answer questions that he did not discover for the first time, but which he explored in a useful way. It is as a partner that they will meet him, along a broad line of advance. Along certain points of that line they will quickly pass his markers and move on, while at other points few will catch up with him.

Finally, however, if we are to do justice to the promise of Teilhard, we must recognize that he stands firm with men who are concerned with the future survival of the planet and its global human community. He is in the "united front" in behalf of the human race that he spoke of in 1936—a front that has confidence in the future and is unqualifedly committed to action that will make the future actual. He is in the intellectual wing of that front, to be sure, but he insists that what we need most is not treatises, not resolution of theological and philosophical complexities, but men who will serve as examples, a community of men who are struggling to make actual the hopes they hold for a more fully human existence.

Key to Abbreviations

The following abbreviations are used for books by Teilhard or about him that are quoted in the text. The references are always given in parentheses following the quotation itself. Publication details are found in the bibliography. The dates given below indicate when the work was originally written, except in the case of essays that appeared over a number of years.

DM	*The Divine Milieu* (1926)
FM	*The Future of Man*
HU	*Hymn of the Universe* (1916-1923)
MPN	*Man's Place in Nature* (1949)
Oe, VI	*Oeuvres de Pierre Teilhard de Chardin,* vol. 6
PM	*The Phenomenon of Man* (1938)
SC	*Science and Christ*
Cuénot	Claude Cuénot, *Teilhard de Chardin, A Biographical Study*
Speaight	Robert Speaight, *The Life of Teilhard de Chardin*

Notes

Preface

1. Georges Crespy, *From Science to Theology: An Essay on Teilhard de Chardin,* p. 79.

Chapter I. Pierre Teilhard de Chardin—Fully Man

1. Speaight, p. 11.
2. Ian Barbour, "Five Ways of Reading Teilhard," *The Teilhard Review,* III (1968) 1, pp. 3-20.
3. Speaight, pp. 136 f.
4. Christopher F. Mooney, *Teilhard de Chardin and the Mystery of Christ,* p. 209.
5. Theodosius Dobzhansky, "Teilhard de Chardin and the Orientation of Evolution," *Zygon: Journal of Religion and Science,* III (1968) 3, p. 258.
6. *Ibid.*
7. Robert Faricy, *Teilhard de Chardin's Theology of the Christian in the World,* p. 40 n.
8. Barbour, *op. cit.,* p. 16.
9. Arthur Knodel, "A Gentile's View," in Robert Francoeur (ed.), *The World of Teilhard,* p. 88.
10. *Ibid.,* p. 90.
11. Dobzhansky, *loc. cit.*
12. Victor Ferkiss, *Technological Man: The Myth and the Reality* (New York: George Braziller, 1969), p. viii.

Chapter II. "A General Significance in Events"

1. Crespy, *op. cit.,* pp. 47 ff.
2. Cuénot, pp. 229 f.
3. *Ibid.,* p. 213.
4. *Ibid.*
5. *Ibid.,* pp. 228 f.

6. George Riggan, "Testing the Teilhardian Foundations," *Zygon: Journal of Religion and Science*, III (1968) 3, pp. 259-313.

7. See the works already cited by Barbour and Dobzhansky; also see Robert Francoeur (ed.), *The World of Teilhard*.

8. These considerations should guard us against the frequently simplistic judgments concerning Teilhard's "Lamarckianism."

9. See *The Future of Man*, chapters XV and XXI; also *The Vision of the Past*, Chapter XIX.

10. Riggan, *op. cit.*, pp. 272 f.

11. Dobzhansky, *op. cit.*, p. 252.

12. See William Saslaw, "Entropy and the Universe," *The Teilhard Review*, III (1968) 1, pp. 76-79.

13. Ferkiss, *op. cit.*, p. 252.

14. John Kenneth Galbraith, *The New Industrial State* (New York: New American Library, 1968); Leroy G. Augenstein, *Come, Let us Play God* (New York: Harper & Row, Publishers, 1969); Michael Harrington, *The Accidental Century* (New York: Macmillan Co., 1965); Theodosius Dobzhansky, *The Biology of Ultimate Concern* (New York: New American Library, 1967); Theodore Roszak, *The Making of a Counter Culture* (Garden City, N.Y.: Doubleday & Co. [Anchor Books], 1969); Paul R. Ehrlich, *Population Bomb* (New York: Ballantine Books, 1968).

15. See, for example, Joseph C. Hough, Jr., *Black Power and White Protestants* (New York: Oxford University Press, 1968), Chapter 1.

16. See the comments by James Dorsey and James Foy in Francoeur, *op. cit.*, Chapters 6 and 10.

17. See Alfred North Whitehead, *Symbolism: Its Meaning and Effect* (New York: G. P. Putnam's Sons [Capricorn Books], 1959) and *Process and Reality: An Essay in Cosmology* (New York: Harper & Row, Publishers, 1960); S. C. Alexander, *Space, Time and Deity* (New York: Dover Publications, 1966); Eric C. Rust, *Evolutionary Philosophies and Contemporary Theology*.

18. Dobzhansky, *The Biology of Ultimate Concern*; John R. Platt, *The Step to Man* (New York: John Wiley & Sons, 1966).

19. See, for example, Julian Steward, "Cultural Evolution Today," in Kyle Haselden and Philip Hefner (eds.), *Changing Man: The Threat and the Promise* (Garden City, N.Y.: Doubleday & Co., 1968), pp. 49-62.

Chapter III. "An Irreversibly Personalizing Universe"

1. See the works listed in the bibliography.

2. Dobzhansky, "Teilhard de Chardin and the Orientation of Evolution," *loc. cit.*, p. 256.

3. Crespy, *op. cit.*, pp. 119 ff.

4. *Ibid.*, pp. 104-113.

5. *Ibid.*, pp. 106 f. See also Faricy, *op. cit.*, pp. 107-112.

6. Crespy, *op. cit.*, pp. 106 f.

7. *Ibid.*, pp. 108 f. See also Mooney, *op. cit.*, p. 144.

8. Crespy, *op. cit.*, p. 113.

9. Albert Camus, *The Myth of Sisyphus and Other Essays,* p. 3.

10. *Ibid.*, p. 21.

11. *Ibid.*, p. 28.

12. Albert Camus, *The Plague*, pp. 117 f.

13. *Ibid.*, p. 116.

14. *Ibid.*, p. 261.

15. The Chicago *Sun-Times*, May 18, 1969

16. Schubert Ogden, *The Reality of God and Other Essays*, Chapter 4.

Chapter IV. The Action That Super-Humanizes

1. Quoted in Speaight, p. 161.

2. Quoted from "Comment je crois," in Henri de Lubac, *Teilhard de Chardin: The Man and His Meaning,* p. 136. Note de Lubac's lengthy discussion of this passage.

3. Speaight, p. 289.

4. Mooney, *op. cit.*, p. 49.

5. Camus, *The Myth of Sisyphus*, p. 121.

6. Roger Garaudy, *From Anathema to Dialogue*, p. 71.

7. *Ibid.*, p. 23, quoted from Karl Marx, *Theses on Feuerbach*, XI.

8. *Ibid.*, p. 92.

9. *Ibid.*, p. 111.

10. *Ibid.*, p. 107.

11. Mooney, *op. cit.*, Chapter 1.

12. Peter L. Berger, *The Sacred Canopy: Elements of a Sociological Theory of Religion* (Garden City, N.Y.: Doubleday & Co., 1967), p. 181.

13. Crespy, *op. cit.*, p. 106.

14. *Ibid.*, p. 76. See also Mooney, *op. cit.*, p. 197.

15. See George Maloney, *The Cosmic Christ, from Paul to Teilhard.* Also, Ian Barbour's sections on Teilhard in his *Issues in Science and Religion.*

16. Crespy, *op. cit.*, p. 74.

Epilogue

1. Crespy, *op. cit.*, p. 165 f.

2. See, for example, in the most recently published collection of

Teilhard's essays, *Science and Christ*, the footnotes on pp. 181 and 185. See also the series of articles by Jerome Perlinski, under the title "The Unpublished Works of Teilhard de Chardin," in *Theoria to Theory*, beginning in III (1969) 4, pp. 62-66.

Bibliography

I. **Writings by Teilhard in English translation**. (The official edition of the complete works is being published in eleven volumes by Editions du Seuil in Paris as *Oeuvres de Pierre Teilhard de Chardin*.)

The Divine Milieu. New York: Harper & Row, Publishers, 1960.

Letters from a Traveller. New York: Harper & Row, Publishers, 1962.

The Future of Man. New York: Harper & Row, Publishers, 1964.

Building of the Earth. Wilkes-Barre, Pa.: Dimension Books, 1965.

Hymn of the Universe. New York: Harper & Row, Publishers, 1965.

Letters from Egypt. New York: Herder & Herder, 1965.

The Making of a Mind. New York: Harper & Row, Publishers, 1965.

The Phenomenon of Man. 2nd ed. New York: Harper & Row, Publishers, 1965.

The Appearance of Man. New York: Harper & Row, Publishers, 1966.

Man's Place in Nature: The Human Zoological Group. New York: Harper & Row, Publishers, 1966.

The Vision of the Past. New York: Harper & Row, Publishers, 1966.

Letters from Paris. New York: Herder & Herder, 1967.

Pierre Teilhard de Chardin, Maurice Blondel, Correspondence. New York: Herder & Herder, 1967.

Letters from Hastings, 1908-1912. New York: Herder & Herder, 1968.

Letters to Two Friends, 1926-1952. New York: New American Library, 1968.

Writings in Time of War. New York: Harper & Row, Publishers, 1968.

Science and Christ. New York: Harper & Row, Publishers, 1969.

Letters to Léontine Zanta. New York: Harper & Row, Publishers, 1969.

Mortier, Jeanne, and Marie-Louise Auboux. *Teilhard de Chardin Album*. New York: Harper & Row, Publishers, 1966.

II. **A select list of books and articles about Teilhard**

Almagno, Romano. *A Basic Teilhard Bibliography*. New York: The American Teilhard de Chardin Association, 1968, 1970.

Barbour, George B. *In the Field with Teilhard de Chardin*. New York: Herder & Herder, 1965.

Barbour, Ian G. "Five Ways of Reading Teilhard," *The Teilhard Review*, III (1968) 1, 3-20.

. *Issues in Science and Religion*. Englewood Cliffs, N.J.: Prentice-Hall, 1966.

. "Teilhard's Process Metaphysics," *The Journal of Religion*, 49 (1969) 2, 136-159.

Crespy, Georges, *From Science to Theology: An Essay on Teilhard de Chardin*. Nashville, Tenn.: Abingdon Press, 1968.

Cuénot, Claude. *Teilhard de Chardin: A Biographical Study*. Baltimore: Helicon Press, 1965.

Dobzhansky, Theodosius. "Teilhard de Chardin and the Orientation of Evolution," *Zygon: Journal of Religion and Science*, III (1968) 3, 242-258.

Faricy, Robert. *Teilhard de Chardin's Theology of the Christian in the World*. New York: Sheed & Ward, 1967.

Francoeur, Robert (ed.). *The World of Teilhard*. Baltimore: Helicon Press, 1961.

de Lubac, Henri. *The Religion of Teilhard de Chardin*. Garden City, N.Y.: Doubleday (Image Books), 1968.

. *Teilhard de Chardin: The Man and His Meaning*. New York: Hawthorn Books, 1965.

Maloney, George A. *The Cosmic Christ, from Paul to Teilhard*. New York: Sheed & Ward, 1968.

Martin, Sister Maria Gratia. *The Spirituality of Teilhard de Chardin*. Paramus, N.J.: Paulist/Newman Press, 1968.

Mooney, Christopher F. *Teilhard de Chardin and the Mystery of Christ*. New York: Harper & Row, Publishers, 1966.

Murray, Michael H. *The Thought of Teilhard de Chardin: An Introduction*. New York: Seabury Press, 1966.

Neville, Robert C. "Nine Books by and About Teilhard," *Journal of the American Academy of Religion*, XXXVII (1969) 1, 71-82.

Perlinski, Jerome, "The Unpublished Works of Teilhard de Chardin," *Theoria to Theory*, III (1969) 4, 62-66.

Poulin, Daniel. *Teilhard de Chardin: Essai de bibliographie* (1955-1966). Quebec: Les Presses de l'université Laval, 1966.

Raven, Charles E. *Teilhard de Chardin, Scientist and Seer*. New York: Harper & Row, Publishers, 1963.

Rideau, Emile. *The Thought of Teilhard de Chardin*. New York: Harper & Row, Publishers, 1967.

Riggan, George A. "Testing the Teilhardian Foundations," *Zygon: Journal of Religion and Science*, III (1968) 3, 259-313.

Rust, Eric. *Evolutionary Philosophies and Contemporary Theology*. Philadelphia: Westminster Press, 1969.

Speaight, Robert. *The Life of Teilhard de Chardin*. New York: Harper & Row, Publishers, 1967.

de Terra, Helmut. *Memories of Teilhard de Chardin*. New York: Harper & Row, Publishers, 1964.

Towers, Bernard. *Teilhard de Chardin*. Richmond, Va.: John Knox Press, 1966.

Tresmontant, Claude. *Pierre Teilhard de Chardin, His Thought*. Baltimore: Helicon Press, 1959.

III. A select list of books that pertain to the topics mentioned in this book to which Teilhard's work is most pertinent

Bergson, Henri. *Creative Evolution*. New York: Modern Library, 1944.

Braaten, Carl E. *The Future of God*. New York: Harper & Row, Publishers, 1969.

Camus, Albert. *The Myth of Sisyphus and Other Essays*. New York: Alfred A. Knopf, 1955.

. *The Plague*. New York: Alfred A. Knopf, 1948.

. *The Rebel: An Essay on Man in Revolt*. New York: Alfred A. Knopf, 1954.

Dewart, Leslie. *The Foundations of Belief*. New York: Herder & Herder, 1969.

. *The Future of Belief*. New York: Herder & Herder, 1966.

Dobzhansky, Theodosius. *Mankind Evolving*. New Haven, Conn.: Yale University Press, 1962.

Garaudy, Roger. *From Anathema to Dialogue: A Marxist Challenge to the Christian Churches*. New York: Herder & Herder, 1966.

Hartshorne, Charles. *The Divine Relativity: A Social Conception of God*. New Haven, Conn.: Yale University Press, 1948.

Meland, Bernard E. *The Realities of Faith*. New York: Oxford University Press, 1962.

Novak, Michael. *Belief and Unbelief*. New York: Macmillan Co., 1965.

Ogden, Schubert M. *The Reality of God and Other Essays*. New York: Harper & Row, Publishers, 1966.

Ogletree, Thomas W. (ed.). *Openings for Marxist-Christian Dialogue*. Nashville, Tenn.: Abingdon Press, 1969.

Pannenberg, Wolfhart. *Theology and the Kingdom of God*. Philadelphia: Westminster Press, 1969.

Robinson, John A. T. *Exploration into God*. Stanford, Calif.: Stanford University Press, 1967.

Sartre, Jean-Paul. *Existentialism and Humanism*. London: Methuen, 1948.